NICHOLAS C. ROSSIS

EMOTIONAL BEATS:

HOW TO EASILY

CONVERT YOUR WRITING

INTO PALPABLE FEELINGS

To the wonderful friends I've made on this journey. I hope these notes are as helpful to you as they have been to me.

CONTENTS

Give me a beat

In some ways, writing resembles painting. You, the artist, find the perfect subject and capture it on paper as best as you can. As with painting, this can be done in either broad brush strokes, or fine ones. The detail can be photographic or minimal. And the materials used can make all the difference between a masterpiece and a run-of-the-mill product.

To add emotion, painters use color. Some buy the best colors they can find on the market; others mix them themselves. Like descriptions in a book, paintings can be vibrant or subdued, depending on the emotion the artist wishes to convey.

To achieve the same effect, genre writers use colorful words. One of the best tools available to us is **beats**. Google defines beats as follows:

"Beats are descriptions of physical action—minor or major—that fall between lines of speech to punch up your dialogue. When a character raises an eyebrow or furrows his brow, this action, or beat, interrupts the dialogue and telegraphs a change in the character's emotional state."

Beats are especially useful in the context of the familiar "show, don't tell" guideline. This collection of some of the best beats I've come across can be a genre fiction writer's best friend. When you struggle to think of a novel way to convey an emotion without naming it, simply check out these handy lists for inspiration and start writing!

Name that emotion

"Show, don't tell," everyone says.

Why?

Because of the way our brains are wired. If you don't name the emotion you are trying to describe, the emotional resonance is actually much stronger. As soon as you name an emotion, however, your readers slip into thinking mode. And when they think about an emotion, they distance themselves from the actual experience of feeling it.

So, the next question is, *how*? How can we show anger, fear, indifference, and the whole range of emotions that characterize the human experience?

Until a few years ago, the answer might have been simple: add an adverb. For example:

He fearfully stepped onto the ladder.

This is simple and unassuming. But, for today's author, unacceptable. "Lazy writing," your writing coach would say, suggesting instead that you use a beat. For example, you could describe your character's actions along the lines of:

He placed one uncertain foot on the ladder and raised his body. Will it hold, *he wondered. He closed his eyes for a second, expecting the worn step to give way. When it didn't, he placed his second foot on the next step. His temples felt damp. He resisted the urge to wipe them, his fingers clutching instead the railing even harder. The ladder held. So far.*

Much better, right? It is richer; immediate; deeper. It draws the reader in; makes them want to read more.

Let's see another example:

Sally felt anxious.

This is a perfect example of a sentence just begging for a beat. So, how about using one to show us instead of telling us?

Sally clutched the hem of her dress, then forced herself to release it and straightened the fabric with long, nervous strokes.

Isn't that more engaging? Still, there is a little more fun to be had.

Tag! You're it.

Beats are great when used as an alternative to dialogue tags. Instead of using the tired ol' *"he said-she said,"* you can use a beat to indicate whose turn it is to speak. Adding dialogue to the previous example, is there any doubt it is Sally doing the talking?

Sally clutched the hem of her dress. "I don't know." She forced herself to release the dress and straightened the fabric with long, nervous strokes. "I really don't know."

You can use beats this way not only to avoid excessive dialogue tags, but also to color dialogue with any sort of emotion—in the case of poor Sally, nervousness.

Talking Heads and How to Avoid them

Talking heads are like comics with nothing but heads and dialogue balloons, placed on a white background. There is no action nor settings; just dialogue.

Not me, you say. *I have lavished page upon page of detailed descriptions of the surroundings.*

And yet, if you have no activity within the dialogue, you can still cause a sense of disengagement between the environment and your characters.

Author **Elizabeth George** mentions the following goals of such activity:

- To keep a scene from showing talking heads;
- To reveal meaningful insights about characters by showing something interesting they are doing;
- To reveal something key about the plot;
- To bring depth by having the activity be a metaphor or something symbolic in the story.

So, keep in mind that your beats can do much more than pace the dialogue. Try to avoid using nothing but the simple, "she sipped her tea" variety: as George points out, beats are most effective when they reveal something about the character or the plot.

How to use this book

I'll let you in on a secret: my first drafts are full of telling and dialogue, with nothing in between but nods, shrugs, and frowns. Which makes for rather terrible writing.

That's because I only care about telling the story. Turning it into an engaging read is left for the second draft. And that's where beats come in.

When I first started writing, I struggled to imagine the right beat for every situation. So, whenever I came up with a great one, I wrote it down for future reference. I did the same when I read a beautiful beat by another author, and went, "what a great way to show X emotion."

It wasn't long before I started jotting down beats and ideas onto a helpful document, imaginatively enough titled "help.doc."

This book contains some of the best beats I have found or written. These are listed first by emotion, then by body part. The next parts include various lovely generic beats and extra information I have come across.

You can use these as inspiration when in search of the perfect dialogue beat. Use them as a way to avoid talking heads. Use them to color your writing. Use them as a shortcut to start polishing that terrible first draft. By building your own beats around these, I hope you find them as useful in your writing, as I do in mine.

PART 1: FEELINGS AND EMOTIONS

Anger

Many of anger's physical reactions are also common to both fear and anger—for example, the heart beating faster. The following beats, however, are particular to anger:

Eyes

- He shot her a venomous look.
- He shot her a furious glance.
- She speared him with another glare.
- He shot a glare up at her to silence her.
- She shot him a glare, but there was still a twinkle in her eye.
- She looked him in the eyes and he looked straight back into hers.
- He held her gaze for a moment before looking away without a word.
- A groan accompanied the roll of his eyes.
- His eyes were stormy.
- Her eyes widened.
- He glared at her without blinking.
- Darkness crossed his eyes.
- She skewered him with an unflinching look.
- Accepting the glaring anger that poured from her eyes, he kept her tight against him.
- Her eyes darkened.

- Her angry gaze sliced his face.
- She flayed him with her gaze.
- He leveled a glowering look.
- She shifted her angry glare to his face.
- She met his unrelenting stare.
- His eyes burned fanatically.
- She gave him a look designed to peel his hide.
- Her eyes flashed with anger.
- Her eyes narrowed to crinkled slits.
- She skewered him with a look.
- She shot him a sour look.
- He shot a glare at her.
- She treated him with a look of unmitigated fury.
- She caught him in a dark gaze.
- His eyes squeezed into thin slits.

Face and Head

- Boiling with fury, he ground his teeth and clenched his jaw so tight, it hurt.
- An infinitesimal twitch in her lips that told him he had hit the mark.
- His nostrils flared.
- He could hear the blood rushing through his head.
- His jaw clenched.
- He gritted his teeth so hard, his jaw ached.
- He ground his teeth.
- Her head flew back.
- He gritted his teeth for control.

- Heat burned his cheeks.
- Anger spiraled from the pit of her stomach.
- Anger swelled in her guts.
- Anger churned in her chest.
- She snorted with derision.
- Her frustration bubbled at her face.
- His expression grew turbulent.

Hands

- His hands dropped to his sides to form clenched fists of tension.
- Her hands squeezed/tightened into fists.
- She clenched/balled her fists.
- He slammed his hand on the table.
- She pounded her fist on the table.
- He shoved back his chair and slammed his fist on the table.
- He slammed his fist on the table, his nostrils flaring.
- His palms stung from digging his fingernails into them.
- He gripped the arm of the chair.
- Her nails cut into the heel of her hand as she tightened it around the bar.
- She wagged her finger at him.
- He jerked a thumb in her direction.
- His fingers drummed the mattress.
- With a swoop of her arm, she flung the stone in a shallow arc.
- He tapped his foot.
- She stomped her foot.
- She pumped a fist.

- He thrust his fists in the air.
- She punched the air.
- She extended her middle finger toward him.
- He gave her the finger.
- She let the door slam in her wake—just enough of a bang to register one final protest.
- Her fists drew up like angry stones.
- Her slap rang loudly in his ears; his cheek throbbed at the suddenness of it all.

Voice

- He howled.
- She hollered.
- He barked.
- She bellowed.
- She roared.
- He cried out.
- She grunted.
- "No," she rasped.
- "No," she exploded.
- "No," she snapped at him.
- He spat the words out through gritted teeth. Frustration and disdain were wrapped up in his instruction.
- "Listen to me," he said, emphasizing each of the last three words.
- She spat out the words.
- ...he said in a croaky voice.
- A twinge of anger laced his voice.

- He grated.
- He started to speak, but huffed out a breath first.
- She choked out.
- His voice/response was laced with irritation/impatience/frustration/anger.
- He growled.
- He retorted.
- He shot back.
- He snapped.
- He panted.
- He groaned.
- He snarled.
- He stammered.
- He exhaled a groan rivaling a rusty hinge.
- Every statement emerged as a growl.
- "What?" he barked in answer.
- He flung a handful of words at her through the open window.
- ...she mumbled, sucking back the bitter taste of past rejections.
- The man's laughter dumped hot coals into the pit of her belly.
- Something bitter dripped from her tone.
- Her voice caught an angry swath through the air.
- She swore, tasting the bitter words. Their immediate heat burned her tongue and she worked her mouth to savor their rough, jagged edges.
- ...he said, his voice a sharp bite.
- A hushed tone wedged itself between his words.
- ... she hissed like a cornered serpent.

Desire

Many of the reactions mentioned in surprise, fear and nervousness may also be present with desire; for example, an increased heart rate; a reddening of the cheeks; talking faster etc. Here are some physical reactions pertaining to desire alone:

- A low and pleasant hum warmed his blood.
- Her brain fizzled.
- She forgot her left from her right.
- Her thoughts wouldn't line up. Every time she tried to align one, it tumbled down, scattering the rest.
- She imagined herself melting, just sliding onto the floor in a puddle of hormones and liquid lust.
- Thinking about it gave her sharp palpitations.
- Those feelings took over and turned her mind to mush.
- The thought turned her mind into a buzzing mess of static.
- She clasped him to her.
- Her face lit up.
- Every hair on his scalp stood to attention, every skin cell tingled, every neuron fired.
- Warmth spread across his chest.
- His heart pounded hard as she finally came to a halt before him, inches from his face.
- ...he said, his breath tickling her ear.
- ...she asked, her voice a bare whisper in the night.

- With a crooking of her index finger, she beckoned him over.
- ...his body draped all over her.
- He brushed his hand across her cheek.
- She tapped a finger on his lips.
- He grabbed her hand and brought it to his mouth, pressing a soft kiss to her knuckles.
- She hooked an arm.
- She gave him the thumbs up.
- She put her hands on her hips.
- She rested a hand on his hip.
- ...she said in a husky voice.
- The heat from his hand burned her skin.
- Desire burned a hot spot in the pit of her belly, until his grin doused her heat.
- He flung a high-ended wolf whistle at her.
- His name felt smooth against her tongue, slightly cool. She licked her lips, as if savoring its sweetness.

Blushing

- She felt the heat of a blush on her cheeks.
- He felt the heat of shame.
- Scarlet heat caressed/warmed her cheeks.
- Her cheeks burned hot scarlet.
- The boy's cheeks pinked up a nice deep shade.
- Her cheeks flushed.
- Her cheeks went hot with that scarlet burn.
- A lovely scarlet flush colored her chocolate complexion.
- Her cheeks flushed warm red.

- That familiar scarlet heat warmed her cheeks.
- His cheeks pinked up real nice, like a schoolgirl's.
- A warm girlish blush pinked his cheeks. I caught his eye and his pink went full-on scarlet.

Eyes

- He stopped abruptly, first looking at the ground, then letting his gaze drift up to her face.
- He was unable to peel his gaze off the woman.
- She did a double take as they passed.
- Her eyes bored into his.
- He wrenched his gaze away.
- All eyes shifted straight to her.
- He sighed, moving his blue gaze to blink up at the ceiling for a few silent moments.
- His eye caught on a sight that brought him up short.
- She closed her eyes and summoned a deep breath, holding it in, then looked blindly skyward.
- She stopped and faced him, holding him by the shoulders as her green eyes bored into his soul.
- ...he said, his eyes rapt on her face.
- His gaze cut to hers.
- His gaze whipped to hers.
- She goggled him.
- He snapped his gaze away.
- His sharp gaze landed on her.
- He angled a glance down at her.
- He dragged his hawkish gaze.

- Her eyes caressed him.

- His gaze cruised her figure.

- His gaze dipped to her.

- Her gaze lingered over him.

- She lowered her eyes.

- His penetrating gaze probed her face.

- She perused the sea of faces [in hopes of…]

- He plugged his eyes back into their sockets.

- She pried her eyes off him.

- He studied her with piercing scrutiny.

- She gave him a subtle wink.

- She swung her restless gaze.

- She tracked the man's gaze.

- She unglued her eyes from him.

- Her eyes strayed to his face.

- He watched until distance obscured her features.

- His gaze devoured her beauty.

- His eyes implored.

- She ignored his appraising glance.

- She cast him an astute gaze.

- She ignored his crudely insulting stare.

- His eyes held her hostage.

- His magnetic eyes were liquid pools of desire.

- He noticed the tears pooling in her eyes and he faltered.

- His gaze penetrated the mist in her eyes.

- His sharp gaze landed on her.

- He angled a glance down at her.

- Her gaze cut sideways.

- She slid a curious glance.
- He lifted his head, pinning her with a feral look.
- His eyes brimmed with warmth.
- The sparkle in his eyes spelled mischief.
- Her eyes tripped up on the sharp angles of his face.
- His dark liquid eyes swore to memorize every part of her.

Hair*

- He played with the silky tendrils of her hair.
- She tossed her head. Her hair whipped wildly, sending droplets of cold water all over the place.
- She flattened down a tuft of his hair.
- He reached out a hand to brush a lock of long hair away from her face.

Also, check out hair in <u>Fear and Nervousness</u>

Kissing, Hugging, Other Beats

- Bringing their mouths within the same breathing space…
- He broke away.
- He skimmed his lips along the sweep of her cheek.
- His lips were meshed with hers.
- His lips entwined with hers.
- Their lips met.
- She met his tongue and gave it teasing laps with her own.
- Her lips were swollen from all the kissing.
- She sank into his body instantly, the hard planes of his muscles enfolding her.

- He swung her up into his arms as he slogged his way out of the water.
- He reached out and bracketed her waist, rubbing the arc of her hip bones with this thumbs.
- Her collarbone left a pool of shadow in which he buried his mouth.
- A quick tug put her sitting pretty on his lap.
- Goosebumps clothed her bare skin.
- His lips brushed her ear, raising goose bumps across her skin.
- I hugged him like that hug had always been inside of me, waiting to come out.

Fear and nervousness

People in danger may experience fear first, followed by anger. This follows the usual flight vs. fight reflex. As a result, you may wish to mix these two up. Keep in mind that people may also try to hide or fight their fear or nervousness (of course, the reader knows better than to fall for that).

Body

The whole body can also be used in a beat. Consider for example the overused "he turned around." Here are some common gestures that come as a response to fear:

- She whirled around.
- He spun around.
- She twirled.
- He pivoted his body.
- She swung her body.
- She straightened her back.
- He tensed.
- He pulled away.
- She jerked away.
- She reeled.
- She shifted back in her seat, as if this made it easier to shift her thoughts.
- Every muscle went rigid.

- She needed to run, to scream, but her body had become petrified stone.
- His muscles froze.
- His words grew legs, kicked her hard in the belly, drove all the breathable air from her body.
- Her posture went limp, as if all her bones had dissolved away, leaving only her skin to make due with standing.
- Panic swelled up inside me, threatening to swallow me belly-first.

Breath

- She gasped.
- She drew a sharp breath.
- He drew in a long breath.
- She took in a deep breath.
- Her breath caught, and then she exhaled in a series of short breaths.
- Her breath hitched a little.
- She drew in a stuttered gasp.
- She drew up a shallow breath.
- Her breath exploded from her mouth.
- His breath quickened.
- She panted.
- She was breathing hard.
- His chest rose and fell with rapid breaths.
- She held her breath.
- He let out a harsh breath.
- She drew in a frustrated breath.

- He drew in a stuttered gasp.
- He drew up a shallow breath.
- She bit down on sour anger.
- A desperate gasp clipped the silence.
- Her breath snagged hold on something inside her chest.
- Damp breath mingled with her words.

Clothes

- She straightened her dress with long, nervous strokes.
- He plucked at the cuff of his shirt.
- She picked a piece of lint from her sleeve.
- He adjusted the lapels of his jacket.
- He tugged at his shirt collar.
- He adjusted his tie.
- She smoothed down the hem of her skirt.
- He yanked the hem of her skirt belly-high.

Eyes

- His eyeballs seemed to sag out.
- He rubbed his eyes with the base of his palms. His hands stopped the rubbing motion and he pushed them deep in his sockets.
- She broke eye contact.
- Her eyes popped wide.
- Her eyes bulged with fright.
- She said nothing, just stared at him blankly while chewing the inside of her mouth.
- Her eyes flew open.

- She froze, eyes wide, struggling to comprehend.
- She rubbed her eyes.
- He found an oil spot on the floor and focused on it until the stain changed shape many times over.
- Her gaze pushed and pulled at all the uncaring faces.
- Her frantic gaze stumbled through the bare parlor, searching for escape.
- He bit down hard on her with his gaze.

Face, head

- A scream sliced through the fog in her brain.
- His pallor grew noticeably.
- The blood drained from her face.
- A panicked expression flittered across his handsome features.
- Her face twitched.
- His face soured.
- She cringed.
- She grimaced.
- She glowered.
- She attempted to let out a scream, but her throat had seized up.
- Fear prickled her scalp.
- His already pale visage grew leached of any color.
- Despair gnawed at her guts.
- Her breath stalled.
- His skull seemed to shrink.
- Oxygen fled his brain.
- Fingers covered his mouth as if to hold the fear/scream inside.
- He screeched/screamed/yelped/gasped.

- She breathed through her open mouth.
- Her head was full of fog.
- Concern marred his features.
- She scratched a vague itch on her nose.
- He rubbed his face with both hands. When he dropped his hands back onto his knees with a slap, his hair was sticking up where he had ruffled it and his eyes looked wide, if not a little manic.
- She closed her eyes and summoned a deep breath, holding it in. Turning her head a fraction, as though straining to hear the notes of a song playing softly in the air, she looked blindly skyward.
- She looked like someone had just walked over her grave.
- Her voice whipped him back.
- Her face was blotchy, as if she'd been crying.
- He looked away and delicately pinched the bridge of his nose as he closed his eyes.
- Tears streaked down her face.
- She scratched her nose/head.
- He rubbed his forehead.
- She pinched the bridge of her nose.
- She cringed.
- He shuddered.
- She flinched.
- She shivered.
- She trembled.
- His body shook.
- She cowered.

- She shrank away from him.

- He huddled in the corner.

- She stiffened.

- She pulled a face of shock.

- She wrinkled her nose, stuck her hip out and folded her arms.

- He whipped his head around to face her.

- She jerked her head back.

- She turned her face away.

- Her mouth was bone dry.

- Fear etched his features.

- She rubbed her temples.

- Her head bobbed nervously.

- Nervous whispers and giggles fluttered freely in the hot air.

- Her head went to wagging back and forth.

- She worked up one of those smiles the simpleminded get for no particular reason.

- His tongue darted out of his mouth to lick his dried lips.

- Blood and all its heat left her face and settled in her feet.

Hair

People often play with their hair when nervous (keep in mind that they may also do this when flirting). For example:

- She ran her hand through her hair.

- He threaded a hand through his hair.

- He raked his fingers through his hair.

- He shoved his hair back away from his face.

- She toyed/played with a lock of hair.

- She twirled her hair.
- She wrapped a curl around her finger.
- She tucked a lock of hair behind her ear.
- She undid her ponytail and shook out her hair.
- She tossed her hair.
- He buried his hands in his hair.
- He stroked his beard.
- He scratched his beard.
- A chilling voice raised the hairs on the back of her neck.
- Every hair on his scalp stood to attention, every skin cell tingled, every neuron fired.
- The hairs on the back of his neck kept tingling in a way that signified he was being watched.
- The fine hairs on the back of her neck stood on end.
- His words brought up the hairs on the back of her neck.
- The hairs on his arm itched beneath his cotton shirt.
- He stabbed his fingers through his hair.
- His hair was disheveled from raking his fingers through it repeatedly.
- He rubbed his fingers through his hair like his head had a pain deep inside.

Hands

- She drummed her fingers on the table.
- He tapped his fingers on the table.
- He fidgeted.
- She rubbed her hands on her thighs.
- An icy panic started to creep up his extremities and into his chest.
- She tugged at her earlobe.
- He bit a nail.
- She chewed on a cuticle.
- She picked at her nails.
- She inspected her fingernails.
- She fiddled with her earring/bracelet.
- He twisted the wedding ring on his finger.
- She played with her cell phone.
- He wrung his hands in front of his body.
- Raising her hands, she momentarily hugged herself.
- He folded his hands in front of him on the table.
- He folded his hands over his chest/over his vest.
- She shoved her hands in her pockets.
- He jammed his hands in his front pockets.
- She folded her arms.
- He crossed his arms over his chest.
- She hugged herself.
- He wrapped his arms around himself.
- He moved his elbow to scratch an intolerable itch in the crook of his arm.

Heart and blood

- His heart pounded hard in his chest.
- Her heart beat so fast, she thought it would pop out of her chest.
- Her heart leaped like a wild stag in her throat.
- Her heart rate kicked up a notch.
- Her heart was rapping against her ribs, ringing in her ears.
- Her heart beat like a drum in her chest.
- Her heart thudded in her chest.
- Her chest heaved in and out.
- His chest heaved to the point that he groaned with each breath.
- Fear clenched like a tight first around her chest.
- His heart thudded louder and louder.
- A weight seemed to press on her chest, robbing her of breath.
- A tendril of panic seized his chest.
- The ache in her chest almost seemed to explode then.
- Panic engulfed him.
- His heart thumped against his rib cage. It fought for space in his chest with the air frozen in his lungs.
- His heart beat double-time.
- It made his blood boil.
- It made his blood curdle.
- His heart felt like a fist pounding the inside of his chest.
- Her heart kicked a ruckus in her chest, mingling fear and excitement with her blood.

Laughter

- He let out a joyless/mirthless chuckle.
- She gave a nervous laugh.
- He broke into a mirthless laugh.

Legs and feet

- He paced up and down the room.
- She shifted from one foot to the other.
- He swayed on his feet.
- She jiggled her foot.
- He swung his leg.
- She shifted her weight against the floor.
- She crossed her legs.
- She dragged her feet.
- She shifted her weight between feet and rocked from side to side, like a boxer keeping his muscles warm before the bell.
- He rocked on his heels, considering his reply.
- He took an involuntary step backward.
- Panic set me atop a pair of shaky twigs that used to be my legs.

Other

- A thousand ants seemed to crawl over her skin.
- A cold shaft of fear assailed her, so powerful that she sank down in her chair.
- Air stalled in his lungs.
- Fear trickled like ice water through his veins.
- He felt as if the walls had shifted closer.
- Ice coated his skin.
- The horror that whiplashed through her wasn't faked.
- Unease rolled through him like a chilled, dark wave.
- Warning bells went off, but he nodded.
- Her skin felt prickly.
- It made his skin crawl.
- Behind us, shadowy figures shifted in the dim setting.
- She tried to snatch hold of his words and make sense of what he meant.
- She stewed in the salty broth of disappointment.
- Rough edges of panic pricked her soul.
- His voice came low, cold.
- Promises and panic mingled with her salty tears.
- A threat spilled from her lips.
- Angry black/red butterflies crowded her sight.
- Her words fell shaky and clipped.
- Smoky black rage flung her across the loft.
- Fear stretched her voice high and tight.
- She brushed the creases from her jacket.

Physical symptoms

These are some of the things that may happen when a person is scared or nervous:

- They may feel hot or cold, may shiver or sweat.
- The breathing changes. Usually it becomes faster and shallower, though for some people it may deepen and slow down.
- The palms may become damp, the mouth dry, the stomach tight, the throat clogged.
- The voice may change: A rushed voice. An off-pitch laugh. A voice that breaks, drops or raises in pitch; a change in speech patterns.
- Micro hesitations may show fear: delayed speech, throat clearing, slow reaction time.
- A forced smile, laugh or verbally agreeing/disagreeing in a way that does not seem genuine is common. This is usually because of so-called **cancelling** gestures: smiling but stepping back; saying *no* but reaching out, etc. Other things that may indicate false smiles include a lack of eye contact or purposefully ignoring someone or something.
- A closed body posture is also a tell: body shielding, arms crossing chest, using the hair to hide the face, etc.
- Nervous people may increase their personal space, e.g. by withdrawing from a group, sitting alone etc.
- Some may try to place furniture (e.g. a chair) between them and whatever scares them.

- A person's hands may fiddle with items, clothing and jewelry, or smooth out items. A person may also perform self-soothing touches to comfort.
- People may hide their hands in some way (e.g. put them in their pockets). This may be because their hands are shaking.
- A stiff posture and movements is common, as the person will remain *too* still and composed.
- Alternatively, they may rush away (the flight instinct kicking in), or make excuses to leave or avoid a situation.
- Sweating or trembling is common, as is a tautness in the muscles or jaw line.
- Nervous people may either grow inanimate and contribute less to conversation, or else talk non-stop and faster than usual.
- Passive-aggressive responses are common; for example verbal responses that seem to have double meanings or sound sarcastic.
- People may attempt to intimidate others into dropping a subject.
- Overreacting to something said or done in jest is also a common tell of nervousness.
- There may be tightness around the eyes or mouth. This betrays the strain of keeping emotion under wraps.
- Fear can make a person yawn, although this may also suggest boredom.
- The skin reacts. There may be goose bumps. The little hairs may stand up in some places. Often, there's an itch, most commonly on the head, though it can occur anywhere. This itch may be very inconvenient when someone tries hard not to move.

- The stomach may clench, churn, or feel like it's filled with ice.
- Smokers may desperately crave a cigarette.
- Some people feel fear in strange places; e.g. the fillings of their teeth hurt.
- During prolonged apprehension, pressure on the bladder builds, resulting in an urge to use the bathroom. In moments of panic, the bladder may open. In a state of terror, the bowels may loosen.
- It might sound like a cliché, but you *can* see your life flash before your eyes.
- People in dangerous situations may have a bitter taste in their mouth. Their sense of smell may be amplified, and they open their nostrils as much as possible to try and catch any whiff of danger. In the face of danger, people may freeze at first, then react aggressively a moment later.
- The heart beats faster; harder; louder. The person may hear or feel their own heart beat in unusual places: in their ears, in their throat, in their mouth.
- Breath is loud in one's ears.
- People may feel stiff, frozen, or unable to move.
- People may flatten their back against a wall, trying to make themselves invisible.
- Their stomach may tighten and feel twisted up inside.

Shivers

- The sound set off an avalanche of uncontrollable shivers.
- He fidgeted as though chills were running up and down his spine.

- Trembling in her grief, she stared blindly away, wiping errant tears.
- A feverish chill tingled down his spine.
- A chill touched the base of her spine and travelled all the way up to her scalp.
- A shiver spiraled down his spine.
- Goose pimples shivered down her spine.
- A chill tiptoed down her neck.
- Chills chased up his back.
- An icy chill curled up his spine.
- She felt a tingle up her spine.
- A chill sauntered down his spine.
- Fear skittered up his spine.
- A rush of fear mingled with his blood.
- A chill coiled up her spine.

Smile

- He scoffed.
- He smirked.
- The corners of her mouth curled upwards into a sneer.
- Bloodless lips twisted in a mockery of a smile.
- A thin-lipped mouth curled into a sneer.
- The thin line that was his mouth curled with sadistic pleasure.
- She plastered on a smile.
- He chuckled halfheartedly, a forced smile playing at the corner of his lips. The mirth didn't reach his eyes.
- A little cocky smirk appeared on her face.
- He sneered [made a mocking grimace].

- His mouth twisted into a smirk.
- She managed to turn the corners of her mouth upward and give half a nod.
- His face divided into a nervous grin.
- His smile fell away.
- She offered one of those forced smiles meant to conceal disdain.
- His grin came lopsided, like the two sides of his face couldn't agree on any one particular expression.
- His grin went snakelike.
- A nervous smile played along the edges of her full lips.
- He hung a lopsided grin on his face.
- He twisted his grin into a smirk.
- The tip of his tongue traced his lips, toning down his grin to a fool's smirk.
- Wicked grins curled around serpentine lips; forked tongues tasted the air: a mouse had wandered into their nest.
- Rage murked his gaze.
- A smirk most evil bent his lips.
- A nervous smile broke on his face.
- An insincere grin split his face in two.

Stomach

- Bile bubbled up from his stomach.
- Sick rose to her mouth.
- Gorge rose to his mouth.
- He had to suppress a wave of nausea.

- The ball of worry and foreboding twisted in his stomach like a fist trying to bury itself into his ribcage.
- His stomach tightened.
- His stomach flopped.
- She felt a little rush of butterflies in her stomach.
- She stood there, the butterflies turning to knots.
- Vomit started to bubble from her stomach.
- Tendrils of terror curled into her stomach.
- A ball of fear formed in his stomach.
- His stomach knotted.
- His stomach swelled with fear.
- His stomach tightened.
- A million butterflies took motion inside my belly, their gossamer wings stroking my soul. Then, he spoke and every one of those happy butterflies went still.
- Her belly went tight with knots strong enough to hold back even the wildest of horses.
- Her belly turned to water.
- Panic jabbed hard at her stomach.

Sweat

- A sheen of sweat was visible on her brow.
- Sweat clung to his brow.
- A fine sheen of sweat shone on his upper lip.
- Beads of cold sweat formed on his forehead.
- Beads of sweat popped out on his forehead.
- Her brow perspired.
- He wiped the moisture developing at his brow.

- Cold sweat glued his shirt to his back.
- Cold sweat trickled down her sides.
- The lack of expression on his face belied the sweat trickling down his spine.
- Sweat erupted on his forehead and he shuddered, gripping her arm to keep from stumbling.
- Sweat beaded on his forehead and broke out on his back as he swallowed hard.
- Sweat beaded around his hairline.
- An achingly lonely bead of sweat skittered down my spine until it disappeared against the snug waist of my dress.
- Sweat rushed down her back.
- A lonely drop of sweat sashayed down her spine. It danced with her attention just long enough for her to glimpse him unguarded.
- Sweat trickled down her neck, beaded up along her spine.
- A bead of sweat like a lover's fingertip traced her spine beneath her blouse.

Throat, neck and shoulders

- She tensed her shoulders.
- The sight made the back of his neck tingle.
- Panic clawed at his throat.
- His breath audibly hitched in his throat.
- Her neck was flexing.
- Her face shook as pink rose up her cheeks.
- Bile burned the back of his throat. He inhaled deeply against it.
- Fear clogged his throat.

- His pulse pounded in his throat.

- She felt her sweaty neck.

- He spat to clear the rasp from his voice.

- He swallowed the sudden lump in his throat.

- She swallowed hard at a tangle of words stuck in her throat.

- Angry bile stung her throat.

- A lump got caught in her throat and promised to choke off air.

- Her throat squeezed down on a scream.

Indifference

Indifference can be hard to convey through a beat, because you're really describing the *lack* of a physical reaction. And your characters can only shrug so much before they start looking like they're having a seizure. Some useful beats are:

- She looked down at him through laced fingers.
- She steepled her long fingers together.
- He absent-mindedly cracked his knuckles.
- He dismissed her with a commanding gesture.
- She pressed her hands to her cheeks.
- She made a steeple of her fingers.
- She sent an indifferent glance about the room.
- He cast only the slightest of glances to the woman before focusing back to [object].
- He yawned.

Shrugs

- She gave a one-shoulder shrug.
- She gave a half shrug.
- He lifted his shoulder in a half shrug.
- She sloughed off a lame shrug.
- She sloughed off that hint of doom.
- A flinch issued from her shoulder.

- A quick shrug usurped her intended nod.
- His shoulders flinched a tight/nervous shrug.

Waves

- He waved a hand to indicate he understood.
- He waved at him dismissively.
- He brushed off her complaints with a dismissive wave of his hand.
- With a flick of her wrist, she waved away the question.
- Accepting the inevitable, he nodded to proceed with an unenthusiastic flourish of his hand.
- She gave a dismissive wave of her hand.
- He waved off her words like they were mosquitoes.
- She flung a shooing gesture.

Interest

Commonly used in a romantic setting, these are some nice ways to show interest between characters.

Eyes

- She anchored her attention on…
- For a moment, his eyes hung on the [object].
- He shifted his gaze to the [object].
- His eyes retraced their path to…
- Her eyes darted toward…
- His dark-eyed gaze tugged at her heart.
- He focused his eyes in the distance as if retrieving data from his brain's hard drive.

Hands & Feet

- She spread her arms wide.
- He held out his arms.
- She raised a hand in greeting.
- He snapped to attention.
- He leaned forward, his fingers laced before him on the tabletop.
- He gestured a little too excitedly and nearly toppled off the couch.

- Her index finger made tight circles in the air while she considered his words.
- He pulled himself to his feet.
- He jumped to his feet.
- He waved.
- She held up her hands.
- She gesticulated.
- He waved his hands.
- She clapped her hands.
- He snapped his fingers.
- She held up a finger: Wait!
- She gestured with a thumb.
- He jerked his thumb toward [object].
- She held out her hand.
- He extended a hand.
- She spaced her index finger and thumb a quarter of an inch apart to show him how much she liked him.

Head

- He cocked his head.
- She bobbed her head in agreement.
- He responded with a wink and nod of acknowledgment.
- She raised her chin.
- He lifted his chin.
- She nodded.
- He bobbed his head.
- She tilted her head.
- She inclined her head.

- He jerked her head in the direction of...
- He responded with a curt nod.
- She tucked a long, loose strand of black hair behind her ear.

Relaxation

In a sense, this category is the flip side of fear and anger. Whereas people experiencing fear tighten their muscles and adopt a closed-body stance, untroubled people have relaxed muscles and an open-body posture:

- He unclenched his fists.
- Her arms dropped at her sides.
- He unclutched his chest.
- He leaned against the wall.
- She folded her hands in her lap.
- She clasped her hands behind her back.
- He propped his chin on his hand.
- She rested her chin on her palm.
- She crossed her ankles in front of her.
- She stretched.
- He yawned.
- He puffed out his chest.
- She thrust out her chest.
- She set her palms down flat on the table.
- He rested his hands on the table.
- She set her hands on the table, palms up.
- He leaned back in his chair.
- She hooked her feet around the chair legs and leaned backwards.

- She put her hands behind her head.
- He put his feet on the desk.
- He uncrossed his legs.
- She stretched out her legs in front of her.
- He sprawled out.
- He waited until the door had closed behind him before exhaling a deep and relieved breath.
- A relieved look washed over his face.
- She made a shushing sound to reassure him.
- His toes and fingers burned as they thawed in front of the fireplace.
- Ankles crossed, his long legs stretched out in front of him.
- His hands resting on the saddle, he relaxed into the ambling ride.
- She swung her short legs.
- She folded her calves under her thighs and scooted back.
- She tucked one leg under her.
- He sat, an ankle across his knee.
- He spoke in a relaxed sort of way, his words drawn-out and low.
- Her breath fell out softly from her lips.
- Her chin took rest against her chest.

Neck and shoulders

- She rolled her shoulders to ease the tension in the back of her neck.
- She tried to massage away the knots of painful tension glued to her shoulders.

- She rubbed the base of her neck where her pulse beat in hard spasms.
- He rubbed the back of his neck.
- She rubbed her shoulder.
- He kneaded his shoulder.
- She rolled her head stiffly to work out the kinks in her shoulders.
- He massaged the back of his neck.
- She squared her shoulders.

Joy

Hopefully, our characters will also experience joy every now and then. Here are some creative ways to portray it.

Feet

- She bounced on her toes.
- She jumped up and down in glee.

Hands

- He gave a wave for the merriment to commence.
- She threw her arms open.
- He threw his hands in the air.
- She brushed her palms together.
- He rubbed his hands together.

Laughter

- He let out a guffaw that echoed throughout the great room.
- The silence broke when he broke out into hysterical laughter; a sort of half chuckle, half splutter.
- He laughed; a hearty, genuine chortle.
- A laugh broke from his chest.
- She pressed a hand to her mouth to stifle her giggles.
- She held back her laughter by a hair.
- Giggles tucked neatly into the nooks and crannies of her words.

- She breathed off an easy laugh.
- A burst of giggles stirred her belly and mingled with a thousand butterflies.
- His broad laugh reached his eyes, spreading small lines outward.

Of course, there are plenty of other verbs available. Depending on the context and the intention, you can use any of these with the above beats:

- Tittered.
- Giggled.
- Guffawed.
- Chuckled.
- Cackled.
- Chortled.
- Howled.
- Snickered.
- Snorted.

Smile

- The corners of her mouth curled upwards into a smile / into a wide grin.
- The corners of his lips quirked into a light smile.
- A small grin stole across the stranger's full, red lips.
- An impish smile made his mouth twitch.
- He smiled a lopsided grin at her.
- The flicker of a smile passed his lips.
- She flashed a huge grin at me.

- He beamed a smile at her.
- He gave a little whisk of a smile and continued on.
- His lips parted in a grin.
- ...flashing an innocent smile.
- A wide smile spread across his face.
- A smile parted his lips.
- The smile grew wider until it reached his eyes.
- She smiled from ear to ear.
- A smile broke through his lips.
- He bit his lower lip, trying not to laugh.
- An amused expression quirked up the side of her mouth as she studied him.
- The corner of her lips tugged up in an inviting smile that refused to let him walk away.
- Her usual crooked smile quirked up one side of her mouth.
- A crooked smile touched her lips despite the wistful eyes.
- He quirked a smile.
- A grin creased his face.
- She smirked.
- An involuntary twitch cracked the edges of his mouth.
- His lips curled upwards.
- "Yes?" she prompted, smiling beatifically [blissful happiness, ecstatically].
- He flashed her a grin.
- A smile creased his face.
- He wore a wide grin.
- She cracked a grin.
- He shot me a roguish grin.

- Damn if that frown didn't turn upside down.
- Her brittle smile belied the sentiment of her words.
- His smile fell away.
- ...coaxing a grin from him
- A cocked smile appeared on his thin lips.
- In a flash, her pouting lips stretched into a beaming smile.
- A smile tugged a corner of her mouth upward.
- His smile widened.
- His mouth twisted into a smile/grin.
- She favored his words with a barely visible upturn at the corners of her mouth.
- He allowed himself a grin.
- She winked as she left, winning her a broad grin from him.
- His lips spread and his eyes crinkled in a grateful expression.
- A ghost of a smile crossed his lips.
- His grin returned.
- A smile warmed his lips.
- A satisfied smile raced across her face.
- He pursed his lips together in a faint smile and nodded.
- His grin got caught up in the dim light.
- His laugh came soft, almost girlish.
- Her smile came warm and dreamy.
- A grin curled around her full lips like a lazy cat settling in a puddle of midday sunshine.
- His grin softened into a genuine smile.
- A smile quirked her lips.

Sadness

Characters will often experience sadness. Many will cry (see next), but some may display their sadness with a relaxation of the muscles. For example:

- He hunched.
- She slouched.
- Her shoulders sagged.
- His shoulders slumped.
- She wilted.
- He went limp.
- He yawned.
- The whole world seemed to be moving in slow motion. She felt like she was walking in a dream world; a horrific, nightmarish dream world.
- He heard a roaring in his ears and lost track of what others were saying [this is also a physical manifestation of unbearable grief].
- Her heart stuttered, and there was this falling, spinning-down feeling.
- His face sagged.
- He lowered his head.
- She hung her head.
- She bowed her head.
- Her countenance tumbled into a dark thing.

Crying

Joy, sadness, exhaustion. The reasons behind a character's tears can be numerous. So, what kind of crying is your character experiencing? Here are some common ways of crying, that will allow you to use the perfect word for each occasion*:

- **Bawl:** This is an unattractive, loud crying that is characterized by mutters, truncated, erratic breathing, clenched facial expressions, and a hunched posture.
- **Howl:** This heavy crying results in an inability to speak or produce sounds even resembling words.
- **Lament**: This kind of crying comes from grief, regret or sorrow.
- **Silent Tears:** This is a soft, inaudible crying that does not draw attention. Try to avoid displaying it as a single tear rolling down one's cheek, as this has been overused and is considered a cliché.
- **Sob**: In a sense, this is the opposite of the silent tears. It is heavy crying with a large volume of tears flowing steadily. It does not have to be inappropriately loud, but it is characterized by the noisy intake of breaths.
- **Snivel:** Audible but soft crying. It usually indicates the presence of drool or mucus.
- **Squall**: A loud cry signifying emotional distress. It is usually associated with infants or very young children.
- **Wail**: The distinguishing feature of wailing is the high pitch.
- **Weep:** A gentler version of sobbing. It involves a soft, steady stream of tears.

- **Whimper:** Soft and irregular crying. There are usually few or no tears.
- **Whine**: Crying in distress, or in a high-pitched, complaining manner.

* See also Ways to Describe Crying.

Sighs

- A sigh escaped his lips.
- He released an old man's sigh.
- A groan accompanied the roll of his eyes.
- His shoulders dropped with a sigh.
- He stood there shaking, a low groaning sound bubbling from his mouth.

Pain

What good is a story with no drama? Characters will inevitably experience discomfort. Sure, they can moan and groan to your heart's content, but there are so many better ways of making the pain palpable.

- She tried to prop herself up on her right elbow, but it collapsed under her, sending lances of stabbing pain to shoot up her shoulder.
- He rubbed the stubble on his head, avoiding the tender knot.
- His skull felt like an eggshell.
- His face started to ache. Dully at first, then in hot stabs.
- A dull headache formed behind his brow.
- His expression was drawn in agony, but not over his own pain.
- His legs flared with fiery slices of pain.
- Pain funneled into her heart.
- His arms were covered in bruises, his knees a maze of grazes and cuts.
- His eyes rolled back into his head. His teeth gnawed until his lips bled.
- Spasms racked his muscles until it seemed his bones would snap.
- Her headache was a hostile squatter occupying every inch of her head.
- His expression was drawn in agony, but not over his own pain.

Surprise

Everyone loves a twist, right? Which is why your characters will probably be surprised rather often. Here are some ways to describe that:

- He shot up an eyebrow.
- He whipped his head around.
- "What?" she asked with a tilt of her head, as if listening to music only she could hear.
- She clamped her mouth shut, but her jaw went slack when she saw him. "You!"
- She arched a questioning eyebrow in his direction.
- His face remained a plank of wood, his amazement hidden by a slow breath.
- He raised his eyebrows at her in disbelief.
- His mouth slackened.
- A question kept gnawing at her.
- He gazed to one side as if playing back the memory in his mind.
- Her eyes widened.
- Her eyebrows shot to her hairline.
- Her eyebrows arched.
- Her lips thinned. She craned her neck to get a view of her back.
- Her head whipped around so fast, she heard a *crack*.
- She slapped a hand over her mouth.
- She covered her mouth with her hand.

- She pressed a hand to her throat.
- She slapped her forehead.
- He smacked his forehead.
- He facepalmed.
- She slapped a hand over her mouth.
- Her eyes widened.
- Her jaw slackened.
- He cocked an eyebrow in surprise.
- She looked at him with folded arms and raised eyebrows.
- Her eyes popped wide.
- The subtle rise of his eyebrow put a giggle in her belly.

Worry

A simple "he frowned" is the easiest way to portray a troubled character. It can get overused rather fast, though. Consider instead some of these alternatives to portray worry:

Frowns

- Dissatisfaction plowed his brow.
- Up went his eyebrows.
- One heavy eyebrow slanted in strong disapproval.
- His expression slid into a frown.
- His brow furrowed.
- Her knitted eyebrows told me she did not believe me.
- Her forced nod of agreement told me I had failed to convince her.
- His forehead creased with worry.
- He had a little furrow between his eyebrows as he thought.
- A deep frown crossed / creased his brow.
- He scrunched his nose.
- Her face scrunched up in worry.
- He wrinkled his nose.
- A worried expression marred her face.
- He knitted his eyebrows.
- Her furrowed brow told me she was beginning to worry.
- There was a deep-set frown on her face.

- His eyes narrowed as his eyebrows pulled together.

- His eyebrows drew together in an anguished expression.

- His eyebrows pulled together in question.

- "This is bad," she muttered, lines in between her eyebrows.

- Her brow puckered threateningly.

- His brow furrowed as his mouth turned grim.

- His brow knitted into a frown.

- Bushy eyebrows beetled.

- She furrowed her brow, alarm bells ringing in her head.

- Her forehead creased with concern.

- He knitted his eyebrows together in puzzlement.

- Worry lined his forehead.

- A deep furrow got tangled in his brow.

- His brow furrowed as if ideas bumped headlong into his mind.

- His brows edged close to each other as he spoke.

Signs of trouble

Except for a frown, you can use any of the following to depict a troubled character:

- She rocked back and forth.
- His head lowered, he watched his feet step one after the other, his hands clasped behind his back to keep from trembling.
- Slowly, he rose to his feet and proceeded to walk with hands clasped behind his back.
- He covered his eyes with a hand.
- She pressed her fingers to her lips.
- He held his finger up to his lips.

- He rubbed his chin.
- His face fell the slightest bit.
- She reclined on the sofa and pressed her fingertips against her shut eyes, like they might roll off, should she lose diligence.
- Her spine jerked her upright.
- He forced his spine upright.
- She shook her head as if that would bring her clarity.
- She shook the cobwebs from her head.
- Concern grew on his face as he listened.

PART 2: BODY PARTS

The eyes have it

As the saying goes, eyes are the window to the soul. They are also a writer's best friend, as they can convey a wide variety of emotions. The only thing you need to watch out for is using overworn words: doesn't "he gaped, unable to peel his gaze off the woman" sound better than "he stared at her"?

- Her eyelids fluttered shut.
- A flash of movement caught her eye.
- Her eyes clouded.
- He blinked owlishly.
- She blinked with feigned innocence.
- Her eyes rolled skyward.
- Her eyes wandered.
- Out of the corner of her eye, she saw him.
- She slammed her eyes shut.
- She squeezed her eyes shut.
- Disapproval gleamed in her eyes.
- She gave him an incredulous look.
- She treated him with a look of unmitigated disappointment.
- Her icy gaze stumbled upon him.
- Rheumy gray eyes picked apart the girl's dress.
- His head tossed his gaze this way and that, like he had plenty to say but not enough time to say it.

He looked, she looked

I know it's really easy to say, "he looked at her," but you may also consider some of the alternatives. After all, there are so many other lovely words, like:

- gaze,
- glance,
- surveyed,
- glared,
- raked,
- searched,
- watched,
- scanned
- inspected,
- inventoried,
- probed,
- watched.

How do I look?

An easy way to depict an emotion is to describe the look on a character's face. So, just what kind of looks are there? Here is a selection:

- **Absent**: when your character is thinking of something else, or wishes they were elsewhere.
- **Appealing**: when your character appeals to another.
- **Beatific**: an extremely happy and peaceful expression.

- **Black**: used when your character is angry or unhappy.
- **Bleak**: a cold and forbidding expression.
- **Bored**: like an **absent** expression, only stronger.
- **Brooding**: when your character has something in their mind and is mulling it over.
- **Bug-eyed**: a character who's surprised, or caught unawares.
- **Dark**: much like a **black** expression, this signifies an angry or unhappy character.
- **Deadpan**: a character who's pretending to be serious, when they are, in fact, joking.
- **Doleful**: a sad expression.
- **Dreamy**: much like an **absent** look, a dreamy look signifies that your character is thinking of something else; something more pleasant than their current situation.
- **Etched**: when a feeling is etched on someone's face, it is perceived as intense.
- **Expressionless**: when your character wishes to hide their feelings.
- **Faint**: The opposite of **etched**; a feeling that barely registers.
- **Fixed**: an expression that does not change or look natural. It can signify brain damage, or simply a lack of empathy.
- **Glazed**: it indicates a **bored** character.
- **Glowering**: a furious character.
- **Grave**: a solemn expression. It can indicate a character who's worried or scared.
- **Haunted**: a character who's spooked by something.
- **Meaningful**: characters exchange meaningful looks to avoid putting their thoughts into words.

- **Mischievous**: much like Loki, this is a character who enjoys causing trouble.
- **Mona Lisa**: like the enigmatic smile of Da Vinci's famous painting.
- **Pained**: a character who's expressing something that causes them anguish—physical or emotional.
- **Pitying**: it can indicate genuine pity, but also that your character does not think someone deserves better.
- **Pleading**: when your character pleads with someone to get their way.
- **Poker**: Much like an **expressionless** look, this signifies a character who wishes to hide their feelings.
- **Quizzical**: a character who's confused or surprised.
- **Radiant**: an extremely happy expression.
- **Roguish**: a roguish expression suggests an individual who does not mind doing something wrong, as long as it's not harmful.
- **Sardonic**: a sardonic character makes fun of others and shows them no respect.
- **Set**: like a **fixed** look, a set expression may hide your character's actual thoughts.
- **Shamefaced**: your character feels shame about something.
- **Slack-jawed**: like a **bug-eyed** look, this is a very surprised character.
- **Sly**: used when your character knows something that others do not.
- **Straight-faced**: when something funny has happened, but your character does not wish to laugh.

- **Sullen**: a (teenage, usually) character who is in a dark mood and does not want to talk.
- **Surly:** like **sullen**, this is a character who is upset.
- **Taut**: a nervous or angry character.
- **Thoughtful**: describes someone lost in thought.
- **Tight-lipped**: may indicate someone who is annoyed about something, but also someone who wishes to make no comment.
- **Unblinking**: an intense stare, where a character does not blink at all.
- **Unnatural**: like a fixed look, it can indicate brain damage, or simply a lack of empathy.
- **Unreadable**: like an **expressionless** look, it shows a character who does not wish to share what they are thinking.
- **Vacant**: like **bored** or **absent**, it describes a character who is not paying attention. It may also show someone who can't understand something.
- **Wan**: a very sad and tired expression.
- **Wide-eyed**: like **bug-eyed**, it indicates surprise or fear.
- **Withering**: a withering look deliberately makes a character feel silly or embarrassed.
- **Wolfish**: a character with a wolfish expression is intending others harm.
- **Wry**: a character who thinks something is funny, but not necessarily pleasant.

Facial expressions

Besides the usual way of describing an expression—he had an X look on his face—there is another, more elegant one:

- A relieved look washed over his face.
- She turned to me, her face lighting up as she spoke.
- A shadow came over his face.
- His emotions flitted across his face.
- Darkness crossed his face.
- A pained look marred his face.
- She had a mischievous look plastered on her face.
- Her brittle smile belied the sentiment of her words.

Do you hear what I hear?

Sound is a particularly evocative sense that can be used to bring any scene to life. For example, a single sentence like, "computers beeped, phones shrilled, and printers whirred" conveys all the bustle in a modern office.

- A shutter banged against the frame.
- A car door slammed.
- A dog howled in the distance.
- The motor stuttered and whined.
- The ceiling fan whirred.
- The rope clanked rhythmically against the flagpole.
- Computers beeped, phones shrilled, and printers whirred.
- Waves hissed against the shore.
- Waves thumped against the hull.
- Thunder rumbled.
- The wind whined.
- Rodent feet scurried.
- Water gurgled in the drainpipe.
- A dog barked in the distance.

- On the farm, I heard…
  - the whoosh of cars speeding by on the highway.
  - the wind rustling through the leaves of trees.

- o the crunch and crack of twigs and seeds fallen from the trees under foot.
  - o the sudden banging of a storm door.
  - o the screeching scrape of a tree branch on the metal of the barn.
  - o the clank on the chain on the gate.
  - o the hoot of a barn owl in some tree close by.
  - o the stomp of a horse's hoof.
  - o the tinny thud of a metal feed door being nosed by a horse.
  - o the contented munch of a horse eating.
  - o the patter of feet across the metal roof of the barn [say by a squirrel or a rat].
  - o the whoosh of water into the bucket.

- The wind carried the sounds of...
  - o the announcer's voice for the junior high football game in a stadium close by.
  - o the roar of the crowd.
  - o the drumming of the band.
  - o a goat bleating next door.
  - o the rasping of metal on metal as a knife pulled clear of the block.

- In the city, I heard...
  - o the whir of car tires on pavement.
  - o a short loud blast of a car horn.
  - o police sirens wailing at first near and then growing distant.
  - o car keys jangling in someone's pocket.
  - o the drone of a jet passing low overhead.
  - o skipping shuffle of footsteps on sidewalk.

o a pedestrian coughing.

o the smack of skin against skin [someone being hit].

o the sudden yowl of a tom cat.

o laughter and fake screams from a throng of young people exiting a bar.

o the hiss of spray paint can in the hands of a graffiti artist.

o echoing footsteps in an alley.

o the rattle of trash can being knocked over, rolling.

o the clink of a piece of metal being kicked.

o a Harley rumbling to life.

Out of the mouth...

We all know that "said" is considered the perfect dialogue tag. Still, there are times when someone wishes to convey a feeling through a well-placed verb. Or a beat:

- He started babbling.
- He started prattling off every detail about [object].
- He clicked her tongue.
- He made a tsk-ing noise with his mouth.
- He smacked his lips.
- He spat the words out through gritted teeth. There was frustration and disdain wrapped up in his words.
- His words trailed off.
- She cooed at him.
- Silence enveloped us.
- Beyond that, nothing out of his mouth would sound appropriate, so he left it there.
- "I need more." His voice broke low on the word.
- Her voice spiked upward as she struggled.
- His tone brooked no argument.
- "It—" She broke off, goggling as vicious curses erupted from the rear of the house.
- "Sure," she piped up.
- She choked out.
- She croaked.

- His voice was redolent with good breeding: deep, measured, forceful, and with perfect enunciation. It rang out chillingly over her.
- I stretched out the last word for emphasis.
- He let his voice roll over her. It was pleasingly deep-toned.
- ...he said, his breath tickling her ear.
- ...she said with a windy sigh.
- ...she asked, her voice a bare whisper in the night.
- ...he said, his voice sweet and smooth like syrup.
- ...she said in carefully spaced words.
- ...the men said in stereo.

Breath

Another thing that comes out of a mouth is, of course, breath. Here are some nice breath-related beats:

- He let out a breath he hadn't even realized he was holding.
- With some loud, straining breaths, he [lifted heavy object].
- He waited until [action] before exhaling a deep and relieved breath.
- ...drawing in a frustrated breath...
- His breath came out in small puffs of cold air.
- She exhaled.
- He blew out his cheeks.
- She huffed.
- She snorted.
- His tongue felt fuzzy. He couldn't remember the last time he'd brushed his teeth.
- He caught a whiff of mint.

- He had tobacco-stained teeth that hadn't seen a toothbrush up close in years, and the breath to prove it.
- His bad breath had nothing on his body odor.
- Her breath escaped soft and moist; a sinless sound; a thing almost pure.

Hands and legs

An easy way to show what someone is thinking is through their feet: whatever they're pointing at, that's where their attention lies. Other ways to use hands and legs in your beats include:

- Tenting his short fingers...
- With a flourish, she brandished a letter dramatically.
- He brushed a hand under his nose like a child with a cold.
- His hand jutted out over the edge of the bed.
- He lifted his hands.
- He spread his hands.
- He leaned on one elbow.

Nods, head and back

How about using our characters' entire head to illustrate a point?

- He let his forehead touch the window.
- He got a crick in his neck looking up at her.
- He shook his head as if clearing cobwebs from his mind.
- She ducked.
- He shook his head.
- His head wagged back and forth.
- Her head twisted left and right atop her shoulder.
- Her head nodded like it rested on a rusty spring.
- His head spun like a top.
- His head lay at a right angle, making him look lopsided, like something inside had come loose.
- She tipped her head in his direction.
- His head wagged side to side, in time with the music.
- Her head bobbed a nervous nod, putting her balance in disarray.
- Her head dipped a quick nod.
- His head did a quick bobble.
- He tossed a nod toward the bushes and narrowed his lazy gaze against hers.
- Her nod tipped real subtle.
- Her nod fell heavy, final.

PART 3: OTHER BEATS

Analogies, Metaphors, and Similes

A good analogy is harder to find than... erm... well, it's pretty hard. Unless you have these to help*:

- She slammed against the chair, her adrenal system upgrading from zoned out to Defcon 1.
- The idea of being that close to her hit him like a shot of tequila in a Red Bull.
- She's crazier than a sackful of raccoons.
- It was as futile as carrying water with a knife.
- The food was spread out like a Thanksgiving feast.
- Her comfort zone retreated into darkness, waving farewell with a lace handkerchief.
- His voice was soft as a feather, yet cold as a hungry tomb.
- Her mouth worked soundlessly, the words unable to permeate her brain. Instead, they bounced around her skull like rogue Ping-Pong balls.
- Her apartment looked like a tornado had blown through it and left a couple frat brothers behind.
- Her red blouse was a favorite—the shredded material looked like a yeti had tried to make out with her.
- She had her kitten motor on purr.
- He moved his mouth around her finger as if he were sucking on a piece of candy.

- She was smiling so hard, the corners of her mouth were getting introduced to her ears.
- Fortunately, he cleared his throat, which pulled her back from the lust ledge just in time, before she swan-dived right into the Abyss of Really Bad Ideas.
- It's going to start raining like a cow pissing on a flat rock, so let's cut to the chase.
- The words rang through her head like a cymbal crash.
- ...coming from her mouth gave the words a wasp-sting-like quality.
- The pleasant smell wafted toward me like a snowflake carried by a gentle breeze.
- He swore up and down and in every compass direction he was innocent.
- She climbed the stairs with less grace than a drunken hippo.
- She moved toward him like a skinless snake on broken glass.
- A gossamer dress so fine, that spiders might have sewn it.
- The memory faded from her head like last night's dreams.
- Trees with skeletal limbs, badly in need of a trim, scraped against slate, like oaken nails on the lid of a coffin.
- He looked at the fancy balusters, like young girls at their first dance, all curves and waists and giggles.
- Paintings in vibrant colors covered walls, like small windows into faraway scenery.
- He vanished, like a movement one catches with the corner of their eye, but disappears when they turn.
- The thought dissipated like morning fog at the rising of the sun.
- Soldiers scurried about like ants swarming from a heap.

- They scurried in a frenzy like the desert lizards do when people interfere with their sunbathing.
- The image melted away like mist before the sun.
- Anger like sharp barbs formed on her words.
- The idea melted inside her head like an ice cube on an August sidewalk.
- He sprang up as quick as a sucker punch to a blind man's nose.
- Whispers buzzed though the crowd's tight huddle like hungry mosquitoes in search of a crimson meal.
- She pranced about like a newly-minted deity demanding worship from somebody—anybody.
- He trailed back to her, like a scared hound hoping for table scraps.
- His eyes went as wide as a pair of pies cooling on a windowsill.
- The words tumbled from her lips like loose pebbles bent on disturbing still waters.
- His face blurred like a funhouse mirror.
- His head bobbed like his neck was hanging from a string.
- Insults fell like rocks from an angry mob seeking revenge.
- His head gave in to a tilt that made him look like a hound hearing a whistle for the first time.
- She wondered who had managed to coax a little sugar from that old pillar of salt.
- She rose like a hornet got her on the backside.
- I trickled inside the room like a slow leak.
- Sweet melody dripped from her perfect lips like nectar from a flower. I swear I could almost smell the jasmine behind the soft words.
- Her hands trembled like an old drunk, fresh on the wagon.

- Her heart banged inside her chest like a tiger raging against the cage that stole its freedom.
- Ideas like butterflies fluttered around her head.
- Her fists drew up like angry stones.
- His grin came lopsided, like the two sides of his face couldn't agree on any one particular expression.
- A smug grin took perch on her thin red lips like an ugly vulture.
- He picked her to pieces, like plucking the wings off a nasty old fly.
- All her words grew wings like moths and fluttered a-loose of her head.
- She drifted back to her cot like a pale wisp of smoke.
- She spat his name from her mouth like a sharp tack.
- Ideas bounced inside his head like tiny rubber balls.
- He chewed on some idea or other, gnawing away as if they there were seeds or pulp.
- He hemmed and hawed, shuffled his feet like a petulant schoolboy who doesn't want to confess a wrong deed.
- He sifted words like sand, trying to lessen a blow he never meant to administer.
- She could see the string dangling from his thoughts like a kite caught in a tree.
- Her nose went all wrinkled as if she had caught whiff of a raccoon long dead.
- His words hummed inside her head like a nest of angry hornets some fool poked with a stick.
- She swallowed courage by the glassful, letting the words slip through her lips.

- Her voice rang like a pealing church bell announcing the second coming.
- His eyes went wide and bright, as if in competition with the low-hanging moon.
- She didn't know if she'd call fear, that sharp taste at the back of her throat, but his words swooped down on her like angry swallows coveting a barn.
- He dropped to the ground like a lead mannequin.
- Her hands were as cold as a hot-water bag in the morning.
- The stone was as cold as the drifting snow.
- Her belly was as cold as if she had swallowed snowballs.
- Her lips were as cold as the night winds.
- She floated onto the street like a ballerina on her big debut.
- He waved off her words like they were mosquitoes.
- Her gaze hit the floor like a dropped quarter.
- A rip along the bottom of her bag called to mind some battlefield casualty, like a veteran's scar.
- He grinned like that ancient serpent, tricking foolish Eve all over again.
- He crept across the threshold like a mangy old mutt scrounging for the crumbs of yesterday's supper.
- Liking her came as easy as sipping iced tea on a lazy August afternoon.
- Denials leaped from my tongue like watermelon seeds bent on winning a distance contest. But the words bumped one into another, falling into a pile at my feet.
- His cheeks pinked up real nice, like a schoolgirl's.
- Smoke swirled up like a charmed snake from his pipe.

- Angry words buzzed through the room like hornets threatening with their barbed stingers those evicting them from their nest.
- She stood bare before him, a new Eve; a female Cain.
- She spun hard on me like a top that's lost its center.
- His greed came awful heavy, like a wet wool blanket suffocating, snuffing out the light.
- My words fell dead and brittle like oak leaves in fall.
- His gaze took hold of her, searched her body up and down like she'd only just now appeared from the ether; a dream or a specter looking for something solid to rest upon.
- Secrets swirled around us like spirits of the dead looking in on sins of the living.
- Second thoughts poked and jabbed at him like a sharp stick.
- Long shadows like dirty fingers reached out from between darkened houses forever empty.
- Fear swallowed whole the curiosity I'd foolishly dared sport with.
- A familiar recollection filled the void in my head, spinning memories of…
- His voice came as soft as his brown-eyed gaze.
- He spewed demands as thick as black smoke.
- The little house sported airs of a petulant child demanding a treat despite its naughty doings.
- She rose like a hornet got her on the backside.
- A grin curled around her full lips like a lazy cat settling in a puddle of midday sunshine.
- They drifted inside the house like flotsam wandering away from the actual wreck.

- Nobody could snatch that smile from her lips.

- The darkening sky rumbled like an empty stomach.

- Her gaze sifted him like a handful of loose pebbles.

- He knitted wisdom to logic and strung a fine bunch of words together; lines carrying enough sway to spring a condemned soul from a death owed.

- A bead of sweat like a lover's fingertip traced her spine beneath her blouse.

- Like a benevolent specter from the netherworld, he eased back into the inky black.

- Like a perfect ballerina, she pulled lazy pirouettes behind the true bones of his discontent.

- She drifted toward him like smoke.

- Footsteps in the stairs outside yanked her from the dirty little smudge of her naughty daydream.

- Her dress graced the floor with a pale blue splash like fallen sky. Discarded underpants conjured visions of puffy white clouds.

- He grinned at her like the devil grinned at Eve.

- His grin washed away like chalk drawings in a spring rain.

- Like quiet smoke, her body settled into the narrow scrap of space of the bathtub.

- A jumble of protests meant to plead his innocence came loose from my lips and fell to the floor, scattering into nothing worthwhile.

- Her silence pricked the sticky air and made it bleed.

- Silence sprinkled the room with its ancient dust.

- Silence, heavy as baled cotton, fell in around them, blotting out the happenings on the street.

- Her tongue went dry as toast; her tone cracked against the quiet air.
- He was as nosy as a heated tomcat.
- Suspicion turned the sticky air fearful.
- Lines of smoke swirled from his nostrils like dizzy snakes.
- Smoke, like twin phantom snakes, curled lazily from his nose. Demons they were, peeking through for a curious gawk at what lay ahead of her.
- Inky black butterflies gathered along the edges of her sight, whispering threats of putting out what little light remained.
- His words came out delicate, an easy saying wrapped in a whisper.
- Her voice was so quiet that you could probably drown it out by whistling.
- Her words fell out a frantic mess, like frenzied bees shook loose of their hive.
- Her eyelids gave a flutter like brand new butterfly wings hoping for flight. She fixed on him through a lazy squint.
- His brow furrowed as if ideas bumped headlong into his mind.
- The words lingered in the space between them like the stench of something gone rancid in the heat.
- The name came sour against her tongue, sharp and jagged. She spoke it aloud and cringed at the taste.
- Hushed voices conspired like conniving schoolboys behind the thin door.
- His point jabbed me like the sharp end of a stick.
- The building was designed with a sort of enclosing roof, a Noah's Ark on stilts, offering the added advantage it would

forever be beyond the reach of floods.

- When she sang, he thought that the moonlight had never serenaded the ocean so beautifully.

* Some of these can also be found in respective parts of this book.

Chairs, windows, and furniture

He stood up. She sat down. I don't know about you, but I've had a pretty hard time describing these two simple actions in a non-yawn-inducing way. Until I came across these:

- He sank into his chair.
- She rested her elbows on the table.
- He shifted in his seat.
- She slumped in the chair.
- She shuffled in her seat to better sit upright and rubbed away the tears with the sleeve of her fleecy jacket.
- I sat bolt upright in bed.
- He pulled himself to his feet.
- He raised himself to his feet, with a loud grunt that betrayed his age.
- The boy jumped at his feet.
- He raised himself to his feet, with a loud grunt that betrayed his age. His brow furrowed. *The older you get, the louder the grunt*, he reflected.
- She lowered herself to the bench.
- She sprung to her feet.
- He leaned his chair onto its rear legs. ... His chair fell forward onto all four legs.
- She jolted upright.
- She jumped to her feet.

- She rose from her seat.
- She stood on the cross legs of her stool to look over the bar.
- The chair squeaked and strained under his heavy frame.
- Loud scrapes and creaks echoed in the still room as he dragged the wooden chair on the floor.
- The wooden chair creaked as she shifted her weight on her seat.
- From behind the door, she heard the high-pitched screeching of chairs being shoved around on the tiled floor.
- She pulled the string on the blinds, which closed with a loud *swoosh*.
- The old wooden blinds clacked and clattered as she pulled the cord.
- The cord made a zipping sound as she rolled up the blind, the cloth rustling with the sudden action.
- The metal blinds rattled against the window.
- He ripped open the blinds with a swish.
- The cloth blinds made a pleasant ruffle as she lowered them.
- She put her body down on a chair.
- She approached the ancient rocking chair as if expecting it to skitter away like a scared cat; as if one wrong move and she'd never set eyes on it again. She offered it her back, settled her body gently against that smooth oak chair, got a feel for its perfect rhythm, the familiarity of creaking wood.

Clothes

There are a million different ways to describe clothes, so this is but a tiny selection, with an emphasis on fantasy.

- He pushed the coat down and off of her shoulders and it fell down her arms, pooling at her feet.
- She admired the gossamer robes.
- She lifted the long cloak and held it high. "I used the pelts of rabbits, and sewed them to well-tanned and thin-beaten deer hide."
- She strapped her short sword to her side, where it hung against her left hip. The knife he had given her sat in its sheath on her right hip.
- Tall leather boots graced her feet.
- She wrapped herself in a fleecy sheepskin worked with fine hand embroidery, spider-thin silken threads woven into ancient symbols no longer understood.
- She wore a pair of simple gathered-leather, over-the-knee boots.
- He wore a fitted charcoal-gray pinstripe that had the look of absurdly expensive bespoke.
- She peeled off her jacket, tossed it on a peg.
- His gaze caressed her painted-on red dress.
- She wore olive-green fatigues and a lightweight tank.
- She was draped in a burgundy wrap dress.

- She wore a light green gown with beading covering the bodice and trickling into the skirt.
- She wore a black Chanel suit that was all business and sexy heels that weren't.
- He teased the gown above her head. All at once, a river of plum-colored silk rushed over her arms and down onto the floor,
- It was pure cashmere, but she dismissed it as just a good layering piece.
- She put on distressed jeans.
- He was wearing tight jeans that played up his broad shoulders and slim hips.
- She dressed with some care, donning a lilac-colored dress accented with white satin trim. She left her light brown hair loose but added a ribbon to keep the strands free from her face.
- Clothes can be mired or soiled (mired in dirt)
- He began dressing, stepping into his pants and then reaching for his shirt. Shrugging into it, he turned.
- She set him moving with a smack to the back of his jeans.
- A rip along the bottom of her bag called to mind some battlefield casualty, like a veteran's scar.
- Sawgrass reached across the path and tugged angrily at the hem of her skirt.
- Her dress graced the floor with a pale blue splash like fallen sky. Discarded underpants conjured visions of puffy white clouds.

Doors

He opened a door. She closed a door. Is that really all we can say about doors?

- He tore the door open.
- She slammed the door.
- The doors lumbered shut.
- They filed through the door.
- Doors banged.
- The door crashed open.
- He vanished behind the glossy wooden doors as he swung them shut. She waited until they clicked closed.
- He slammed the door behind him.
- The door creaked open.
- Doors squeaked, scraped and groaned open.
- He reached in and yanked the connecting door closed.
- The door snapped shut.
- Behind her, the door groaned shut.
- The door thudded closed.
- The door clanked into its lock.
- The brass door handle squealed when he pressed it down. The door swung inwards without making a noise. When he closed the door behind him, the handle squealed again, as if in pain.
- The doorbell gave a soulless 'ping'. She heard shuffling steps, then the rattling of a chain, and the door opened, scraping

across the carpet. While she brushed her damp shoes on the door mat, the door clacked shut and the chain rattled again.

- The master key was on his belt. He slid it into the lock and jerked open the door to the cell. The hinge squeaked from the weight of the door.

- The solid wood door they'd so carefully fortified was split in half, like kindling.

- Her fingers found the rain-slick knob and, to her surprise, it turned in her hand.

- His hand found the rust-roughened knob. To his surprise, it turned in his palm.

- Her fingers found the lichen-encrusted knob and, to her surprise, it turned in her hand.

- With a pneumatic hiss, a vertical line appeared on the rock face. The wall split and slid apart to reveal a small area behind it.

- Just as the door was about to latch shut, it stopped moving.

- Every beat of the bronze knocker reflected the beats of her heart.

- He was stopped by a cherry door flanked by stained-glass sidelights and crowned by a matching transom / covered with elaborate wrought-iron latticework.

- Voices broke through the door, warm and loose by tone, although she couldn't piece together any single conversation.

- We broke the threshold and crossed into the sort of scene I'd conjured up during a hundred sleepless nights.

- The door gave up a wide yawn. A short man leaned into the gap.

- His wide shape filled the front door and crept onto the porch.

- She drifted through the open door.

- A coded knock issued from his knuckles.

- The red door pulled a tight yawn. A porcelain face filled the thin crack.

- The doorknob felt cool against her hand.

- He shoved the door closed.

- Hushed voices conspired like conniving schoolboys behind the thin door.

- A curious jiggle found the doorknob.

Driving

I'm sure you can drive just fine. But how easy do you find it to describe your character's driving? These might help.

- He cut across three lanes of traffic, careening over the median to speed back in the other direction.
- She coasted the SUV out onto the road.
- He backed out, hand on the gear shifter.
- We swerved to the right as the back end of the SUV fishtailed until it came to a halt.
- He jammed the car into gear and gunned the engine.
- A red traffic light stopped us.
- A cab screeched to the curb.
- He turned into [name of] Street, tires screeching in protest.
- She pulled onto a sandy road going off into the desert.
- The truck bounced over the rutted road.
- The tires screeched as the truck careened to a stop.
- The truck peeled out of the driveway. She opened it up on the main road.
- She hauled the steering wheel to the left as her right tires careened down the incline.
- Flying through the maze of trees, we hung a sharp right.
- She parked the truck in the gravel patch.
- Traction caught and the car lurched forward.
- He mashed the brake to the floor.

- He stifled the engine's growl and flung his door open.
- The smell of burped gasoline stung her nose.
- First gear submitted with a painful grind.
- The driver's door gave up a squeaky yawn and spit him onto his feet.
- A black Model T Ford skulked in the tall grass beside the lane.
- A dark Victorian villa cast invisible hands toward our car, luring us nice and snug against the curb out front.
- He stamped on the brake pedal.
- The car mounted the kerb.
- She snatched the steering wheel out of his hands.

Fights

Fights. The staple in many a genre. Where would be without them? Here are a few words that may prove useful when describing a fight:

- He crushed his opponent.
- He crashed against the floor.
- She hurled the stone at him.
- He pinned her to the ground.
- He pummeled the shield.
- She splintered the wood.
- She plunged at him.
- She swerved his sword.
- He catapulted at her.
- He wrenched the knife from her hand.
- He was already hurtling toward them.
- He lunged at her, wielding a huge axe.
- He swung his axe.
- He flung his axe at her.
- He dashed / raced / vaulted at them.
- She charged them.
- She hasted toward them.
- He plummeted to his death.
- She pounced at him.
- She dived after him.
- She slapped / thumped him.

- Fists thudded.

- Swords clanked.

- He sheathed his blade in the scabbard on his belt.

- A sudden and forceful tremor sent him sprawling on all fours.

- Furious, she hurled her knife after him. A moment too late, the blade thudded into the wall as its target vanished.

- Blood caked her wound, forming smudged streaks down her thigh.

- Blood was bubbling up through the wound.

- Taking the sword from where it rested against the wall, he sheathed it on his hip.

- He instinctively grabbed the side of his head as a surge of splitting pain pounded within.

- She launched herself into a spinning leap toward her opponent. The man lunged forward to meet her, jabbing his fist towards her stomach. She dodged him nimbly and cracked the pole down on his broad back. There was a sickening crunch, and the man sprawled senseless on the ground.

- She whirled around in a circle, looking for any stragglers.

- A large stream of blood, now caked and hardened, clung to the side of his face. His eyes had a glassy sheen; his expression was dazed. He gingerly touched the wound near his temple, and winced slightly on contact. He flicked a few flakes of dry blood from his fingers.

- A fine sheen of sweat shone on his upper lip.

- A second volley hissed in his ears, quelling the advance.

- As he bolted into the forest, he caught a glimpse of the enemy's warriors, faces smeared with red paint, rushing up the road and pouring into the camp.

- The larger the army, the more logistics needed tending.
- Blood jetted in all directions, hitting him in the face.
- A mushroom cloud boiled over the ocean. The noise and shockwave washed over them.
- His boots scuffed and kicked at the cobbles as he was dragged up onto a high stone step.
- She'd yank all of her hair out.
- His head thunked back onto the blood-streaked cobblestones.
- Blood sprinkled from the wound.
- It was as if she could sense every nerve, cell, muscle, drop of blood and hair in her body individually.
- She shot up to him and grabbed him by the throat.
- The shouts and clangs of metal coming from all around them faded from her ears, as she concentrated on her opponent's eyes, waiting for a tell-tale sign of attack. It came perhaps thirty seconds later. A slight narrowing of his eyes told her he would charge. When he did, she parried, slid from beneath the attack and spun, her sword held ready to defend her. He came again, this time swinging from the opposite direction. She caught the blade on the flat of her own. The force of the blow sent a numbing shockwave along her arm. She back-pedaled quickly and circled to the right to give her arm time to recover. He charged again. She caught the first blow easily and flicked her wrist to separate. This time, he came with an arcing attack. She stopped his blade before he could finish the swing, slipped beneath it and pushed him back. Spinning, he reversed and attacked again, faster than she expected. In the midst of his attack, his eyes flicked to the right. She backed quickly away. He came at her an instant later in a full-out charge. Instead of

back-pedaling, as she knew he expected, she pushed forward, her blade moving in the figure eight, her arms weaving so fast that the blade blurred in the air. She kept her counter attack until he fell into her pattern of weaves and faints. Then he changed pace and pushed her back, his sword hammering steadily in short, swift strokes. Their blades gleamed in the air, the sound of metal echoing loud and crisp until, finally, she spotted an opening in his defensive pattern. She dipped beneath one swing, stepped closer and an instant later touched the tip of her sword to the side of his neck.

- She lifted her bow and notched an arrow.
- With the sun on his back, he raised his arm and whirled his hand in a circle, finishing with a finger pointing forward. Behind him, the voices of the officers echoed his hand signal with commands to move.
- His arm ached from the fighting. His legs cramped, but he held himself strong.
- The mist-like appendages exploded, falling and twisting, as the creature fought for its existence.
- The fighting was fierce; no quarter asked, none given.
- He held his sword high and bellowed the command to reform their ranks. The cry echoed up and down the lines of armored men and women.
- The man bled his life out on the floor.
- He jumped off the crate, rolled beneath the monster, lashed out with his sword, and sliced through one of its legs.
- He swung his arms to loosen them.

Horses

Like fights, horses are a staple of many a genre. Even if not many of them are around nowadays, it pays to know how to describe our heroes' interactions with them.

- He tightened the cinch on the last horse.
- With her bow slung across her shoulder and back, the quiver of arrows attached to the horse's saddle, she pulled on the reins.
- He stroked the horse's powerful neck, being nuzzled at the same time.
- She stroked the horse's wide, flat nose.
- She stroked the horse's neck, dismounted and stretched her body. "I feel like I have spent my entire life on his back," she said, continuing to twist and stretch the kinks that had grown with each mile ridden.
- The horse stood there shaking, a low groaning sound bubbling from his mouth.
- Molten steel coursing through his veins, he mounted the horse, rode the valley floor and marched up the hillside, the horse in tow.
- He yanked the reins.
- He hefted his sword and started his horse into the ravine.
- His hands resting on the pommel, he relaxed into the ambling ride.

- The horse stomped and danced, ears flattened at the tight hold on the reins.
- Leaning forward, he patted the big horse's neck.

Houses and Scenery

The best way to describe a house is to flick through an (online) architectural magazine. The second best is to read on.

- The walls were covered in rich, black wallpaper that exhibited a shimmering, barely perceptible pattern in the winking candlelight.
- Depression glass candleholders stood on the shelf.
- Along the far, short wall was a wide, polished, walnut, rectangular table.
- Their footsteps echoed on the travertine floors.
- All the paint chips he had been forced to stare at had driven him crazy.
- The interior was cuter still, with wooden floors polished to a warm honey-gold and exposed brick walls showcasing vintage travel posters.
- The room was perfect for sit-downs that didn't call for the formality of a conference room.
- The room had seamless windows and a breathtaking view of the park.
- The polished marble flooring gleamed in the full sun.
- Blue plaid curtains accented with a soft beige draped the windows.
- He touched the rain-streaked pane.
- A smattering of trees met his gaze.

- He saw a pretty jut of cliffs upholstered with wild grass.
- The tower lorded over the seaside village.
- Ladders slid on oiled rollers from one section to the next. Bookcases lined each level, from floor to molding.
- The garden was redolent with the scent of gardenias.
- The central desk looked like a cresting wave, scooped up from a thick base on one side, its leading edge flattening to form a workspace.
- Brocaded chairs topped by soft throws lined the wall.
- One section of the gate rolled on a rail to the side and another could be raised and lowered.
- Their footsteps echoed on the gold-veined marble flooring.
- A wet bar was tucked into an alcove. Another wall was nothing but floor-to-ceiling plate-glass windows with French doors.
- Original works of art hung placed on recession-lit walls.
- She touched the embroidered fingertip towels.
- He gazed at the slow-paddling ceiling fans.
- Behind elegant banisters, platform walkways permitted catwalk access on the second and third levels.
- It was a grand two-story home, painted a pristine white and fronted by tall shrubs that sheltered most of the columned porch from view.
- Shining hardwood floors graced a large open space furnished as a combination living and dining area.
- The ceilings were open, the rafters exposed.
- The porch was narrow, but the second story of the cottage pitched over it and provided much welcome cover.
- The shutters outside were open to the sun's indifferent reach, and dawn streaked in.

- Simple railing emerged from the wraparound veranda without any architectural artifice.
- Two enormous English elms flanked the old manor. Their bowing branches arched elegantly over it, bobbing in the gentle breeze.
- The furniture is old-world, sumptuous and expensive, like the authentic tufted Chesterfield sofa.
- Trees with skeletal limbs, badly in need of a trim, scraped against slate, like oaken nails on the lid of a coffin.
- He looked at the fancy balusters, like young girls at their first dance, all curves and waists and giggles.
- Paintings in vibrant colors covered walls, like small windows into faraway scenery.
- Five interior poles held up the roof of the command tent, a standard issue square block of pale canvas. Scraps of rope tied open the doors to admit morning light and a hint of breeze rustled the maps and missives littering the long table. The chief's sturdy chair stood in a corner, stacked with slightly crumpled, rolled documents, a clear indication that the man preferred to stand.
- The road coughed them out into a clearing set beside standing water.
- High trees brooded over the night, keeping back the moon's shine.
- Lilacs scented the warm air; honeybees droned their busy song while picking over those late-summer blooms. Mosquitoes planned attacks from the overgrown grass.

Hunger, drinks and food

Your character will no doubt feel the need to eat and drink on occasion. Here are some ways to describe this:

- He slugged back the last of his drink.
- He studied the amber liquid rolling around his glass as he swirled it.
- She ushered me towards the lounge and laid the snacks down on a large coffee table in the center.
- He placed both mugs down in front of them.
- She took a large swig from her mug.
- He heard the clink of crystal and the shrill of high-pitched feminine laughter.
- He set a bottle down.
- She plonked the bottle onto the table.
- He swished the wine in his mouth.
- He drained his stein.
- He emptied his flask.
- She brought over a flagon of lemonade.
- He slipped out of bed, plodded along to the kitchen, flicked on the kettle and popped two slices of wholemeal bread into the toaster.
- She finished off her toast and the dregs of her brew.
- He poured citron water with floating sprigs of honeybalm.
- He looked up so sharply, he spilt citron water from his beaker.

- He sipped his shots, not tossed them back.
- "Shall I decant?" he asked [pour small quantity to try out].
- She set the Bordeaux glass on the white linen tablecloth and used a foil cutter to remove the foil cap over the cork.
- He poured a dram and swirled it in the tumbler, letting it coat the glass.
- He popped the tab on his beer.
- He spoke into his coffee cup as he took a sip, his voice suddenly lower as if there was someone else in the room who might overhear.
- She slammed her mug down.
- She started gobbling up the delicious [food].
- Tendrils of steam from the tea rose in the cold morning air. She took a cup in both hands, raised it to scent the drink and blew across its surface before taking a sip.
- He blew on his [hot food] and his stomach rumbled. He tasted his food, winced and cooled his burning tongue with a quick gulp of water.
- He speared a cherry tomato and shoved it into his mouth.
- Her stomach gurgled/churned growled in protest.
- He had a tower of stacked glasses cradled in one hand and several bottles precariously trapped between the fingers of his other.
- Ice clinked against the glass. A drop of condensation slid from the rim to the tablecloth, fanning out and growing larger and larger.
- She drew that bottle to her lips, pulled its liquid heat against her tongue, and breathed off those vapors. A cough or two dropped into her lap.

- A liquid rope of warmth spilled eagerly from the bottle, and into his mouth and throat.
- He brought a shot to his lips and sipped at its fire. It burned his throat, turning his blood hot.

Light

One of my hobbies is photography, and I still remember something a photographer friend and teacher once told me: even with the best film and camera, your photograph will only be as good as the light available to you. Here are some ways to capture its infinite variations*:

- The pitiless afternoon sun filtered through the rose-clad lattices, throwing rhombi of light onto the table.
- The sun sent the first shy rays across the plain.
- A few stray rays of sunlight filtered through gauze curtains to caress the wall across him.
- Sunlight fell across the pavement, making the dust glitter.
- A shaft of sunlight split down the middle of the room.
- The slice of light through the door expanded and cut across the floor.
- The crystals took the slanting sunshine and threw brilliant rainbow shards of light onto the ceiling.
- The empty room was draped in shadows that deepened with the onset of dusk.
- He withdrew his green flip-top lighter, the tell-tale 'click-zip' of the lid and striker echoing into the darkness.
- The sky was hinting at sunrise.
- Every once in a while, a streak of runaway light escaped through a gap in the clouds in a feast of fuchsia and orange.
- Dawn painted the sky in party colors.

- Stretching, she watched the sun filter through the trees.
- The low morning light rose like smoke from the night grass.
- The sun was still shining, a beam here and there piercing the gray that lay solidly overhead.
- The river reflected the soft violet of twilight.
- The diving summer sun was still baking the concrete rooftops. In the distance, his house basked under its relentless rays.
- Bands of pink blended into the dark purple of the horizon as the day rose.
- Sharp-angled blades of sunlight sliced open the heavy green canopy above, bleeding lemon-yellow splashes of warmth and light into the cool shade of her private oasis.
- He pulled her into a splash of orange glowing off a candle.
- Cool blue dripped onto the stage from lights burning high above.
- Slivers of afternoon sunlight sliced through the green canopy overhead and left its lemon-yellow glow here and there.
- Evening tossed its gauzy gray over the city, dulling even the silvery shine coming off a low-slung moon.
- He faded into shifting shadows stalking corners where the candles weren't meant to reach.
- The orange flash of a spun lighter scattered those shadows for a moment.
- A kerosene lamp flung its awkward yellow haze against the low-slung ceiling.
- Morning tripped into the room gray and grimy.
- Fire milked an orange glow from a candle burning somewhere in the back.

- Kerosene fed the hungry flame in a lamp atop a modest kitchen table.
- Moonlight spilled in, splashing everything with its silver shine.
- They fell into a puddle of dirty yellow light.
- He watched her undress in a puddle of light coming from his lamp.
- Lemon-yellow sunlight splashed against the pulled share and gave shape to the man on the other side of that locked door.
- Pulled shades blotted out the glow of a gas lamp from the street below.
- Sharp white light stung her eyes.

See also Weather, skies and views below.

Other

Every now and then I come across a lovely beat that is hard to categorize. Here are some of my favorite ones:

- The movers scuffed the wall with the table.
- He was hovering inches from her face.
- She raised the storefront's tattered awning.
- He sang a sprightly melody.
- A rowdy gaggle of youth.
- He frittered his life away.
- Soon, he was lost in the crush of people now spilling out into the streets in droves.
- Behind the curtains came the tapping. The *tap tap tap* rhythm of a branch against the window.
- Now place her in the past, where she belongs.
- The boy looked up at me, his sweet face clouded with an earnestness only the young possess. His big brown eyes shone with anticipation of a story. She smiled, sat forward and took his soft, freckled cheeks in her calloused palms.
- We managed to cajole and wind our way through the throng of people.
- The crowd sang along, clapping and stomping their feet in time with the music.
- Fog covered the forest, like smoky, distant memories.

- As herd after herd departed, the earth rumbled faintly under hundreds of clopping hooves.
- Dashing back to the ladder, she shuffled up the steps quickly. When she hit the metal door, she frantically waved her wrist tag across it.
- …the man said, after a long minute.
- Two green spots, like fiery eyes, penetrated the darkness and raised goose-bumps.
- Her face flushed as she grabbed the bag and slung it on the floor.
- I could see through the crest of the waves to the clean bottom.
- She was always mom first, last and in between.
- I handed the bag over to him and he obediently slung it over his shoulder.
- One woman scooped it up and set it upon the bank.
- I wanted to see how the following few days panned out.
- The cat nuzzled into the warmth of her lap for a while, before she heard his small feet pitter-patter toward the kitchen.
- I was on tender hooks all day long.
- She snapped her bag shut.
- She secreted away the letter as she glided towards him.
- A bucketful of thoughts needed to go, to make room for new ones.
- It was as if she could sense every nerve, cell, muscle, drop of blood and hair in her body individually.
- *A near-death experience, described by Eamon Gosney:* "No actual "Being" presented themselves when I arrived as a night swimmer, floating on a silky sea. However, the very molecules of the air and water were made of love. There was simply no

room for hate, guilt, or fear. Only love. I was preparing to follow a trusted and comforting voice, which said, "All you have to do is float." I was turning to walk into the soft moonlight, but I was brought back at that moment by unbearably bright lights and pain that felt like a thousand razor blades cutting me at once. Had I gone into the light, I suppose the shock paddles would have failed."

- He looked at the line snaking along the street in front of the small restaurant waiting for a table.

- A cupboard creaked open, clanked shut. Steps brushed across a carpet, then an armchair sighed under the weight of a person sitting down. Glass chinked against glass, liquid sloshed. She waited—no toast was spoken, no glass clanked against another glass. He was alone inside.

- He made some crackerjack suggestions.

- He belonged to the much-vaunted warrior class.

- She crossed a refuse-strewn street.

- He slammed his sword back into its sheath.

- He held the spear in his hands. It was a beautiful weapon. The head was made from dark bronze, tapering gracefully into a fine, fearfully sharp point. The edges glittered in the tent's half-light. It was fastened to the haft by thirty rivets of gold. The haft was made of rowan, darkened with age, worn smooth and polished by the grip of many hands through the years. He hefted the spear, testing its weight. It was perfectly balanced, as if made specifically for him.

- Each baby's face puckered and grimaced, and a last feeble protest escaped on its warm milky breath.

- Suddenly, it was all salty kisses and sandy toes.

- He bent down, grabbed the crate and hefted it.
- The iris on the wall started whirling, emitting a laser web that swept back and forth over the wall.
- A joystick control popped up from the control panel. A montage of views from the ship's cameras was overlaid over the cockpit window.
- It was really not so much a book as a thick stack of pages held together with three leather loops.
- He slowly, relentlessly materialized out of the dark, his cloak swishing, his black eyes sparkling with joy, his red lips nuzzling the white, submissive, swooning neck and his incisors, just slightly showing, beginning to glisten.
- He watched himself thinking, as though discovering a new, unfamiliar country where thoughts depended on each other, interlocked. The thought he was handling would fit into the next one he had; he was driving. He had never driven thoughts before. They had come, wanted or unwanted. Now he was telling them where to go.
- The dogs bared their teeth, lips curled, snarling. Sharp claws scratched and clawed at the baluster rods, massive paws attempting to knock me off. The dogs barked, jumped, banged against the railing. White foam dripped off razor-sharp teeth.
- He mock-buffed his fingernails on his inexistent lapel with pride.
- Sweet music leaked into the night. Laughter danced between the notes.
- Smoky fumes choked the air, mingled with the earthy odor wafting up from the river, creating its own unique scent.
- A man's chubby face filled the small peephole.

- He angled them along a narrow row of cages.

- The woman sported a mask of someone broken beyond repair.

- We did a slow trickle into the dark alley, taking to the shadows that promised freedom under their cover.

- A million thoughts rushed my mind, though I couldn't snatch and hold on to any single one.

- His bulk put the creaky floorboards in a complaining mood as he crossed the darkened parlor.

- A lonely tear breached her will and splashed hard against his hand.

- Delicate notes seasoned the night.

- Shiny black hair spilled on to her shoulders.

- Straight black hair washed over her shoulders like spilled ink.

- Saxophone rose high on a warm breeze and sprinkled them with a familiar tune.

- She drew water from that hand pump and filled the tub to halfway.

- His voice came wet with blood.

- Her brown hair was like a living being, held together by Rasta braids that fell to her waist. Curly strands of sun-bleached hair escaped the braids and stood at attention in no particular order away from her head.

- Her skin, the color of cinnamon, and her fine features made him think of exotic locales and sun-kissed shores.

- Her sole item of jewelry, a ring on her index finger, had a large, sparkling, see-through, medium blue stone.

- Depending on the kind, bells will:
    - tinkle and jingle (sleigh bells),
    - ring and chime (wedding bells),

- o clang (alarm bells),
- o toll and knell (funeral bells).

Seafaring

A few seafaring-related beats:

- Below her, the stormy waters of the ocean rose and fell with a thunderous crash, while torrents of rain cascaded downward in slanting, wind-driven sheets. On the horizon, ships sailed in a formation like birds flying south. They bobbed upon the waves, their sails billowing under the strain of harsh winds. The powerful winds were pushing them toward their destination faster than expected.

- The ship skimmed over the water, picking up speed on its race toward shore. The sails billowed fully, propelling the ship faster. Four minutes later, the ship ground to a stop, its bow embedded in the gravel-like sand of the cove's shore. Cries and shouts rose from the deck.

- From shore to horizon there was nothing but angry, churning gray slashed by whitecaps that looked keen-edged enough to slice through a hull.

- Beneath them, water dropped at least four hundred feet down, churning in monstrous eddies and spitting up foam.

- She caught glimpses and stretches of the turbulent blue sea as it spewed against a wide, sandy curve of beach.

- The sea foamed against the sand, dotted with boats, rough or calm and every mood in between.

- Beneath us, angry black water swirled and spat, demanding respect from anyone foolish enough to wander along its muddy banks.

- Boat whistles of differing octaves competed for attention down on the river. Paddlewheels slapped at the murky water. Seamen hollered orders meant to be followed.

Walking and moving (I)

There are so many ways of describing walking, each of them conveying a certain emotion. For instance, consider the differences between the following: walk; tread; stride; stroll; saunter; march; amble; stagger; perambulate; ramble; meander; wander; dawdle; mosey; roam; rove; travel; journey; tramp; trudge; slog; plod; lumber; scramble; journey; shuffle; hobble; shamble; waddle; trundle; limp.

Here are some more examples:

- He swung around/spun around.
- She slinked over to him
- She hurtled into the room with all the momentum of a tidal wave, slamming the door behind her.
- He rushed to his feet.
- He barreled into the room
- Snake: I look up at the silhouette snaking towards me
- He lumbered down the hall.
- He fled the room.
- He stalked off.
- He stormed out of the room / he stormed off.
- He stomped down the hall.
- He rushed down the corridor.
- She sashayed off behind the curtain.
- She tottered along, unsteadily in her high heels.

- He tumbled down the alleyway.
- They followed her as she wove through the room.
- I'd better scurry.
- He flew out of the room.
- He slogged his way back into the room.
- Their boots crunched across the snow as they walked.
- His head lowered, he watched his feet step one after the other, his hands clasped behind his back to keep from trembling.
- His feet kicked up small drifts, ribboned by the wind. He needed this trek to sober up, his head feeling stuffed with wool and crowded with too many thoughts.
- He shooed her from the room.
- She stomped down the hallway to her bedroom and slammed the door behind her.
- He dawdled for a while, alone in the empty room.
- He made a beeline for the bar.
- He hoisted the satchel farther up his shoulder and continued walking.
- He fell into step beside her.
- He headed past her.
- He stepped off the elevator with purpose.
- He took four ground-eating steps.
- She backpedaled, heading for her boots.
- She slinked down the darkened corridor.
- They made their way through...
- He propelled me toward the far wall.
- She marched up to him.
- She stalked into the kitchen.

- She strode past him.
- He stormed across the parking lot.
- He made a break for the door.
- He loped forward into the thick fog.
- She picked her way over the rough ground.
- She slogged through a quicksand jungle.
- She strode forward.
- He thrust past him, shouldering him roughly aside and flinging hard against the palisade.
- He walked towards her, cresting the shingle ridge.
- She stepped away.
- She drew nearer.
- He leaned closer.
- She inched forward.
- He loomed closer.
- The children bounded down the stairs for dinner.

Walking and moving (II)

For maximum effect, you can combine the beats above with some of the verbs below, most of which were found on <u>WriteWorld</u> (<u>http://writeworld.org/</u>):

- **Amble**: to walk easily and/or aimlessly.
- **Bounce**: to walk energetically.
- **Caper**: to skip or dance about in a lively or playful way.
- **Careen**: to pitch dangerously to one side while walking or running.
- **Cavort**: to jump or dance around excitedly.
- **Clump**: to walk heavily and/or clumsily.
- **Creep**: To move quietly and slowly.
- **Cross**: To cross a road or street.
- **Falter**: to walk unsteadily.
- **Flounder**: to walk with great difficulty.
- **Foot it**: (slang) to depart or set off by walking.
- **Footslog**: to walk heavily and firmly, as when weary, or through mud.
- **Gimp**: to limp; hobble.
- **Hike**: to take a long walk, especially in a park or a wilderness area.
- **Hobble**: to walk unsteadily or with difficulty; see also *limp*.
- **Hoof it**: (slang) to walk; see *foot it.*
- **Leg it**: (slang) to walk; see *foot it.*

- **Limp**: to walk unsteadily because of injury, especially favoring one leg; see also *falter.*
- **Lumber**: to walk slowly and heavily.
- **Lurch**: to walk slowly or furtively, as if stalking someone.
- **March**: to walk rhythmically alone or in a group, especially according to a specified procedure.
- **Meander**: to walk or move aimlessly and idly without fixed direction.
- **Mince**: to walk delicately.
- **Mosey**: see *amble*; also, used colloquially in the phrase "mosey along."
- **Nip**: (British English) to go briskly or lightly; also used colloquially in the phrase "nip (on/out/over/round/down/in)" to refer to a brief trip to a certain destination, as if on an errand.
- **Pace**: to walk precisely to mark off a distance, or walk intently or nervously, especially back and forth.
- **Pad**: to walk with steady steps making a soft dull sound.
- **Parade**: to walk ostentatiously, as if to show off.
- **Patter**: to walk or run somewhere, making a series of short quiet sounds with your feet
- **Perambulate**: see *stroll*; to travel on foot, or walk to inspect or measure a boundary.
- **Peregrinate**: to walk, especially to travel.
- **Plod**: to walk slowly and heavily, as if reluctant or weary.
- **Pound**: to walk or go with heavy steps; move along with force or vigor; see *lumber.*
- **Power walk**: to walk briskly for fitness.
- **Prance**: to walk joyfully, as if dancing or skipping.

- **Promenade**: to go on a leisurely walk, especially in a public place as a social activity; see *parade.*
- **Prowl**: to move around an area in a quiet way, especially because you intend to do something bad
- **Pussyfoot**: to walk stealthily or warily.
- **Ramble**: to walk or travel aimlessly.
- **Roam**: to go without fixed direction and without any particular destination, often for pleasure; see *ramble.*
- **Rove**: to travel constantly over a relatively lengthy time period without a fixed destination; wander.
- **Sashay**: to glide, move, or proceed easily or nonchalantly; see *parade.*
- **Saunter**: to walk about easily.
- **Scuff**: to walk without lifting one's feet.
- **Scuttle**: to run off.
- **Scurry**: to hurry away.
- **Shamble**: to walk or go awkwardly; shuffle; see *scuff.*
- **Shuffle**: to walk without lifting the feet or with clumsy steps and a shambling gait; see *scuff.*
- **Skulk**: to move in a stealthy or furtive manner.
- **Slink**: to go somewhere slowly and quietly so that people will not notice you.
- **Slip**: to go somewhere, especially quickly and quietly without people noticing you or stopping you.
- **Slog**: to move in a slow, heavy manner, as if carrying a weight.
- **Sneak**: to move somewhere quietly and secretly so that no one can see you or hear you.
- **Somnambulate**: to walk while asleep.
- **Spring**: to jump out on someone, surprising them.

- **Stagger**: to walk unsteadily.

- **Stalk**: to walk stealthily, as in pursuit.

- **Steal**: to move somewhere quietly and secretly.

- **Step**: to walk, or place one's foot or feet in a new position.

- **Stomp**: to walk heavily, as if in anger.

- **Stride**: to walk purposefully, with long steps.

- **Stroll**: to walk in a leisurely way; see *saunter.*

- **Strut**: to walk with a stiff, erect, and apparently arrogant or conceited gait; see *parade.*

- **Stumble**: to walk clumsily or unsteadily, or trip.

- **Stump**: to walk heavily, as with a limp; see *lumber.*

- **Swagger**: to walk with aggressive self-confidence.

- **Tiptoe**: to walk carefully on the toes or on the balls of the foot, as if in stealth.

- **Toddle**: to move with short, unsteady steps, as a young child; see *saunter* and *stagger.*

- **Totter**: to walk or go with faltering steps, as if from extreme weakness; see *stagger*(also, sway or become unstable).

- **Traipse**: to walk lightly and/or aimlessly.

- **Tramp**: to walk heavily or noisily; see *lumber* and *hike.*

- **Trample**: to walk so as to crush something underfoot.

- **Traverse**: to walk across or over a distance.

- **Tread**: to walk slowly and steadily.

- **Trip**: to walk lightly; see also *stumble.*

- **Tromp**: to tread heavily, especially to crush underfoot; see *lumber.*

- **Troop**: to walk in unison, or collectively.

- **Trot**: to proceed at a pace faster than a walk; see *nip.*

- **Trudge**: to walk slowly and with heavy steps, typically because of exhaustion or harsh conditions; see *plod.*
- **Waddle**: to walk clumsily or as if burdened, swinging the body.
- **Wade**: to walk through water or with difficulty, as if impeded.
- **Wander**: to move from place to place without a fixed route; see *ramble.*
- **Weave**: to move in non-linear way, usually in order to avoid several obstacles.

Waking up and beds

Much like standing up from a chair, waking up can be hard to make interesting. Hopefully, these beats will help:

- She snapped awake.
- She jolted awake to the brutal sound of splintering wood and a resounding crash.
- She catapulted out of bed and stumbled across the door.
- Rubbing the sleep from her eyes with one hand and covering a yawn with the other, she shuffled into the corner of the sofa, propping herself against the armrest and the back for support.
- He slipped out of bed.
- She plopped down on her bed and grabbed a pillow to cuddle to her chest.
- She cracked open her eyes and squinted at her surroundings.
- He washed/rubbed the sleep from his face.
- She swung her warm feet out of bed and into cold slippers.
- She hopped out of bed.
- A woman still crumpled by sleep answered the door.
- Her morning voice sounded just as he remembered: a little scratchy from a dry throat and her speech slow, like it was still warming up. She scrunched up her face and yawned.
- ...he said, gaining his feet.
- She rose like a hornet got her on the backside.
- She sat bolt upright and gained her feet.

- Her eyelids gave a flutter like brand new butterfly wings hoping for flight. She fixed on him through a lazy squint.

Weather, Skies, and Views

With our surroundings offering so many interesting views, finding the perfect description can be a challenge. Well, not anymore!

- The mottled sky ranged from mid gray to dirty white.
- A soft breeze picked up her hair, stirring the strands around her cheeks.
- As a warm breeze stirred the sheer curtains of the open patio doors, the scent of baked stone and crushed flowers folded within its balmy caress.
- We watched a thick, fluffy cloud shuttle across the sky.
- It had started to flurry and a thin coating of snow covered the ground.
- Overcast skies turned everything dreary and cold.
- Rain spilled down in sheets.
- The breeze was just a teasing shimmer in the air, fluttering leaves.
- The rising sun shone beneath the lip of the departing cloud.
- The sky was clear and the air carried a light musky scent mingled with pine.
- There was still a bit of bite to the wind.
- We watched a steady deluge of rain.
- The cold seeped in through his light jacket and made him shiver.

- Sharp jets/droplets of icy cold water needled her back. She shivered under the prickly feeling and raised her hand to protect herself from the tiny ice-cold daggers.
- Water lapped against the graveled beach, causing a gentle swoosh as each wave slipped back into the azure ocean. Gulls circled above, calling to each other as they flew effortlessly back and forth. A gull swooped down to land a few meters from where they sat. It looked in their direction and cawed. He waved his arm to shoo the bird away, but it hopped back and cawed once more.
- A squall streamed over the palisades. Dark clouds let forth sheets of rain, while churning winds ripped across the rocks, howling through the crevices.
- In the west, deep pink and purple bands were chased beneath the horizon by the coming of night, while above and in the north, blackening clouds massed.
- The gray sky darkened above the field, turning the rocky ground into shiny, blood-soaked black pools.
- The tall wheat was performing its best impression of a green sea. The wind sent wave after wave to ripple through its surface, as if about to crash on a distant shore.
- Clouds darkened the sky as he ran.
- A flash lit the world white.
- The world flashed to white clarity as another crack of lightning struck.
- The sickle moon was gone from the sky, leaving only a blanket of stars to give light.
- Blossoming dittany spilled over the slope.

- The woman drifted away as the morning fog thinned in the warming sun.
- Black clouds smeared the sky.
- Thick fingers of mist stole across the lake, blotting out the far shore.
- She heard the throbbing pulse of rain.
- The mist twined itself around the trees.
- Tufty clouds scudded across the lake in a reverse image of the heavens, its trembling silken surface spoiled by the ripples her feet stirred. They chased away from her across the mirror, folds in a liquid blanket.
- A rank gust of icy air hit her.
- The hulk of the dark mountains rambled against a sky layered with smoky clouds.
- A red-throated sparrow alighted on the branch above her.
- She found a rock overhang to weather out the now freezing night.
- The stars were feverish.
- Down the slope, water bubbled and purled over boulders, the wild rush complementing her internal turbulence.
- A falcon circled lazily in the bottomless azure sky. It soared on an updraft, hunting.
- She rode south as the sky grew pastel and brightened into full day.
- Hulking masses of architecture hung over her.
- The breeze fluttered leaves growing toward their summer ripeness.
- Flowers grew in abundance, spilling out of window boxes, baskets, pots, and from the dooryards.

- A fitful wind swirled dirt and exhaust fumes into a toxic soup.

- By the time she had left, it was overcast and pouring.

- The sky had gone black with the bruise of thick angry clouds. They expelled a low rumble. A cool breeze tossed her hair into a delicate dance. A lone drop of rain kissed her bare shoulder.

- Jagged silver flashes jabbed the coming night over the horizon.

- The darkening sky rumbled like an empty stomach.

PART 4: EXTRAS

1000 Verbs to Write By

Author Alicia Dean has shared a list called "1,000 verbs to write by" that includes synonyms for some widely used (and overused) verbs.

For "entered"

stepped inside	burst in	intruded
went in	set foot in/on	penetrated
came in	broke in	passed into
sailed in	forced her way in	

For "felt, seemed, showed, looked like"

sensed	connoted	struck her as
had the impression	hinted at	looked as if
understood	alluded to	looked like
detected	implied	had the look of
seemed	intimated	had every appearance
appeared	presaged	of
betrayed	portended	had the earmarks of
indicated	forewarned	resembled
betokened	disclosed	sounded like
foretokened	displayed	exhibited
revealed	lay open	evidenced
bespoke	made manifest	showed
suggested	exposed	manifested
signified	bared	emblematic of

For "had, held"

bore	contained	contained
exhibited	wore	toted
showed	sported	possessed
displayed	spanned	retained
betrayed	suspended	embraced
wielded	grasped	evinced
carried	gripped	
was furnished with	clutched	

For "heard"

overheard	listened in	took in
caught	gathered	gave audience to
detected	heard tell of	gave an ear to
picked up	strained her ears	lent an ear to
perceived	harked	heard him out
apprehended	harkened	within earshot
eavesdropped	attended to	out of earshot
listened	took heed of	

For "hit"

beat	punched	impacted
socked	rammed	attacked
bumped	crashed	hacked
clapped	thwacked	swiped
thumped	slapped	swung
lashed	smacked	trounced

| pummeled | pumped | tackled |

For "jumped"

vaulted	sprang	erupted
leapt/leaped	lunged	exploded
pounced	launched	shot from
startled	jerked	
flinched	jolted	

For "left, exited"

ran off	decamped	quit
walked off	deserted	took off
went out	repaired	fled
departed	retired	sallied forth
retreated	withdrew	bowed her way out
rushed off	stormed off	hurried away

For "lie down, lay"

reclined	lay prostrate	sprawled
eased onto	lay recumbent	lounged
flopped onto	lay back	slouched
lay prone	rested	slumped
lolled	reposed	sunk into
luxuriated	lazed	collapsed on

For "looked, saw"

glared	fixed her gaze on	scrutinized
glanced off	noted	perused
regarded	recognized	sized up
made out	identified	took stock of
descried	took a look	skimmed
remarked	took a glance	glanced through
had in sight	stared	flipped through
glowered	leered	perceived
squinted	scowled	discerned
shot him a look	scanned	beheld
fixed her with a stare	peered	watched for
sighted	squinted	looked on
ogled	gaped	eyed
cast a glance	noticed	detected
his eyes begged her to	observed	contemplated
amplify	considered	kept in sight
gazed	watched	held in view
gaped	viewed	stood guard
spotted	took in	kept watch
surveyed	studied	monitored
turned an eye on	examined	distinguished
looked upon	inspected	

For "pulled"

pulled out	extracted	extricated
removed	produced	lugged

drew	tugged	dragged
took out	yanked	fished out

For "pushed"

propelled	shoved	roused
ballasted	thrust	prompted
set in motion	pressed forward	forged ahead
drove	made one's way	
trundled	squeezed through	

For "put"

stashed	plunked	tossed
placed	parked	threw
posed	stationed	flung
posited	planted	lobbed
plunked down	perched	hurled
mounted	inserted	heaved
positioned	lay	cast
stationed	set	slapped onto
set before	set upright	draped
dropped	stood on end	dunked
crammed	upended	eased
stuffed	deposited	shifted
stuck	consigned	interposed
lodged	relegated	installed
plopped	strapped	

For "reacted"

reeled back	retracted	drew back
rocked back	sighed	stepped back
flushed	exhaled	stiffened
blanched	inhaled	resisted
blushed	flicked	retreated
scowled	flung	raised an eyebrow
nodded her consent	reclined	cocked her head to one side
nodded an agreement	shifted	
smiled	relaxed	put her head to one side
grinned	swallowed	
grimaced	pouted	tilted her head
shrugged and said	looked + adj.	chuckled
admitted with a nod	yielded	yawned
shook his head	hesitated	laughed
beamed	made no attempt to	snickered
smirked	frowned	giggled
simpered	made no answer	stifled a yawn
listed	fell silent	stifled a laugh
tilted	paused	took a deep breath
swayed	stared	glanced off
keeled over	gasped	glared
flinched	started	shrugged
shivered	startled	devoid of emotion
sniffed	slackened	grinned
blinked	reclined	sneered

For "smelled"

got scent of	inhaled	caught a whiff of
sensed	scented	discerned
sniffed	snuffed	reeked
detected	breathed in	stunk
snuffled	savored	assaulted the nostrils
snorted	perceived	

For "stood"

got to his feet	rose to his feet	held herself erect
jumped up	got up	stationed herself
rose	remained upright	

For "tasted", "drank"

savored	melted	quaffed
relished	licked	imbibed
nibbled at	slurped	tippled
tried	chugged	nipped
sipped	smacked	supped
gulped	suckled	drained
took a deep swallow	sucked	washed down
chewed	swigged	swilled down
ingested	swilled	guzzled down
ruminated	chomped	lapped up
sampled	ground	soused
sank his teeth into	munched	quenched

bit into	gnawed	crunched

For "thought, remembered"

wondered	deduced	mused
asked herself	reviewed	ruminated
pondered	pictured	recalled
noticed	featured	mulled over
reflected	imagined	brooded over
struck her as	pretended	projected
entertained a notion	hoped	anticipated
held in one's mind	feared	concluded
It occurred to her	envisioned	esteemed
It came to her	deliberated	took heed
realized	envisaged	kept in mind
knew	called up	guessed
she considered.	conjured up	supposed
she considered this.	conceived of	formed an image of
he was tempted to	fancied	conjured
brought to mind	allowed the conceit	hatched
he was taken with the idea that	judged	fabricated
she reasoned	suspected	fashioned
understood	intended	formulated
considered	expected	concocted
went over	planned	reasoned that
turned it over in her mind	concentrated	acknowledged
	inferred	weighed
	thought back to	reconsidered
flirted with the idea	put her in mind of	thought better of

recollected	called to mind	
bore in mind	reminded her of	

For "took"

drew	elevated	nabbed
withdrew	seized	packed
pulled out a	prized open	ransacked
picked	wrenched	appropriated
selected	wrested	swiped
chose	produced	snared
plucked	extracted	dragged
removed	extricated	acquired
snatched out	accepted	obtained
scooped up	fetched	gained
rooted out	grabbed	procured
snatched	snitched	garnered
trapped	took hold of	gleaned
took up	jimmied	pilfered
raised	gathered	lowered
picked up	grasped	took down
hoisted	gripped	tore down
set upright	fingered	swapped

For "touched"

clutched	patted	probed
pawed	tapped	goaded
gripped	tamped	twisted
grasped	rapped	wedged

took hold of	brushed	pried
adjusted	bedaubed	prized open
felt	dappled	pry/pried
manipulated	dabbed	pulled
maneuvered	swept across	pushed
twiddled	scraped	primped
palpated	glanced	preened
palmed	alighted	rattled
handled	pressed	pumped
thumbed	wrung	mangled
rummaged through	kneaded	massaged
caressed	shoved	felt
fondled	gouged	flattened
stroked	grazed	smoothed
grazed	prodded	scooped up
rubbed	ticked	flicked
tugged	trapped	flipped
squeezed	jabbed	flogged
scratched	poked	fondled
pinched	pressed	groped
handled	tapped	stubbed
held	drummed	scoured
knifed	wiggled	scrubbed
mauled	worked	

For "turned"

wheeled around	swiveled	veered
twisted to one side	reeled	shifted

whirled about	trundled	divagated
rotated	circled	angled off
spun on her heels	eddied	shunted
pivoted	swirled	
revolved	sheered	

For "was, were"

stood	took place	stayed
sat	contained	persisted
took up	spanned	befell (happened)
perched	loomed	bechanced
lay	occupied	occurred
hung	remained	happened

For "walked" or "ran"

paced	continued on	dodged
shuffled	drifted past/along	edged
scuffed	strayed	eluded
lumbered	glided along	escaped
plodded	tramped	evaded
sidled	trudged	fled
slinked/slunk	traipsed	dashed
proceeded	trod/treaded/trodden	chased
wended	limped	hurtled
went on his way	hobbled	swished
shuffled	lurched	swaggered
scuffed	crawled	trotted

scuffled	crossed	scrambled
stumbled	traversed	scampered
shambled	inched across	scooted
waddled	emerged	scuttled
wobbled	entered	scurried
slouched	evacuated	trekked
minced	advanced	strode
strolled	approached	stalked
sauntered	bushwhacked	stomped
ambled	climbed	strutted
marched	crept along, crept away	stamped
stepped		staggered
roamed	sneaked/snuck	tripped
roved	tiptoed	galloped
meandered	stepped lightly	charged
shadowed	pussyfooted	darted
pursued	descended	danced
pranced	ascended	bolted
flitted	rushed	tore
flew	sidestepped	tore along
hauled off	skidded	made rapid strides
groped his way	skipped	covered ground
launched across	stole	sprinted
scaled	steered	careered
lunged	swerved	scudded
moved	veered	hastened
paraded	listed	raced
passed	trampled	hurried
patrolled	ushered	jogged

plowed	waded	cantered
prowled	wandered	loped
propelled	hiked	tripped
pursued	withdrew	took flight
raced	ambulated	decamped
sailed	absconded	
trailed after	drifted	

Describing Death

Author **D. Wallace Peach** has written many of the beats found in this book. She has kindly allowed me to include here her excellent post on how real people react to death.

1. Common **Physical Reactions** to a Death:

    - Tightness in the forehead, throat, or chest
    - Dry mouth
    - Breathlessness
    - Nausea and/or a hollow feeling in the stomach
    - Weakness, fatigue
    - Sleep disturbances, dreams, and nightmares
    - Appetite disturbances

2. **Disbelief** is often a first reaction upon hearing of a death, especially if the death is sudden. Disbelief manifests as an initial numbness, a surreal sense that this can't be happening, that the world has stopped making sense.

3. **Internal/External Coping**: Your characters' reactions will vary widely. Some will express themselves externally, others internally. This can be a source of misunderstanding – the less emotionally expressive characters accused of coldness or indifference, the more openly expressive characters accused of wallowing in self-pity.

4. **Social Immersion/Withdrawal:** Some characters will desire immersion within their social network to gain support or stem loneliness and fear. Other characters may avoid interactions, needing time to process and reflect in solitude. Many will fall somewhere in between, appearing fine until the brittle walls of control collapse at a word or gesture.

5. **The Rollercoaster:** Most people will dip in and out of grief, able to handle it in small doses before backing up and regaining emotional control. Your characters will function and grieve, function and grieve.

6. **Reminders:** Some characters may avoid reminders of the deceased, finding that places or objects trigger painful feelings. Others may have the opposite reaction—desiring to visit those places and carry keepsakes.

7. **Active/Passive:** Death generates a sense of helplessness. Some grieving characters may resort to intense activity (cooking, training, working, painting the house, or shopping). This is a coping mechanism that counters the loss of control. Others will feel lethargic, distracted and forgetful. They'll have trouble focusing or wander in a fog without the will to complete the simplest tasks.

8. **Spirituality and Religion:** For some characters, death may challenge spiritual or religious beliefs and shake faith to its foundations. For others, spiritual or religious beliefs may be or become the lifeline that sees the character through.

9. **Conflicted Relationships:** These are relationships shaped by a tangle of positive and negative experiences, wishes, and emotions. Characters are grappling for balance and control, for respect, love, or approval. Death ends all chances for a satisfactory resolution. The feelings left behind are a stew of love, anger, regret, and guilt.

10. **Recklessness:** Though recklessness may appear as a death wish, it might actually be angry defiance, a wager that death can be beaten at its game. Characters may also put themselves at risk to make up for a failure to protect others or guilt at their own survival.

11. **Anxiety, insecurity, and panic:** Unlike recklessness, anxiety can be paralyzing. A shattered world can leave a character with a heightened sense of mortality, a fear of surviving on their own, or an aversion to taking risks.

12. **Relief:** Characters may feel relief after the death, particularly if the deceased suffered. Relief and a sense of liberation may also occur at the end of conflicted relationship, the battle finally over. Guilt frequently accompanies the sense of relief.

13. **Guilt:** Guilt is very common and often completely illogical. All the "*I should have's*" and "*if only's*" roll through the character's brain, especially in cases of suicide.

14. **Anger:** Anger generally has four sources:

- Justified anger at perpetrators and the failures of individuals and institutions. This is fertile ground for thoughts of revenge.

- Lashing out at others in response to feelings of helplessness and loss of control.

- Anger at one's self for an inability to prevent the death.

- Anger at the deceased for dying, for not fighting harder, not making better choices, or abandoning the survivors (like guilt, this anger isn't always logical).

15. **Unexpected Death:** Death out of the natural sequence of life is generally more tragic than death after a long life. Sudden death is frequently harder to deal with than a loss that's expected. Death by a purposeful or negligent hand is often more difficult than one by accident or illness.

16. **Previous Experience:** Previous experience with death can prepare a character for new losses and soften the sharp edges. At the same time, if previous deaths weren't fully processed, new losses can trigger unresolved emotions and complicate healing.

17. **Delaying grief:** Death and grief make characters feel vulnerable. In dangerous situations, it's common for grief responses to be suppressed or delayed. Then, once safe, the emotional blockade opens. If that safe haven for grief is a long time coming, consider that feelings may bottleneck, turn in on the character, or explode.

18. **Children's Grief:** Don't forget that babies, children, and teens grieve too.

- Babies experience a sense of absence in their lives. They also respond to the stress of the adults around them.

- Little children and teens experience the SAME feelings as adults including guilt – believing that they somehow could have prevented the death.

- Children also dip in and out of grief, cry and whine one minute, then play and laugh the next.

- Children and teens tend to regress to younger behaviors.

- Children will frequently delay their own grief until they see that the adults are handling it well and it's safe to grieve.

- In an attempt to fit in, teenagers will frequently hide their grief. Teens may not talk about their feelings with their parents, but will talk to another trusted adult and among each other.

List of Common Synonyms

Author **Lara Eakins** has painstakingly compiled and shared an excellent list of synonyms for some of the most common words we use in our writing:

Amazing — incredible, unbelievable, improbable, fabulous, wonderful, fantastic, astonishing, astounding, extraordinary.

Anger — enrage, infuriate, arouse, nettle, exasperate, inflame, madden.

Angry — mad, furious, enraged, excited, wrathful, indignant, exasperated, aroused, inflamed.

Answer — reply, respond, retort, acknowledge.

Ask- — question, inquire of, seek information from, put a question to, demand, request, expect, inquire, query, interrogate, examine, quiz.

Awful — dreadful, terrible, abominable, bad, poor, unpleasant.

Bad — evil, immoral, wicked, corrupt, sinful, depraved, rotten, contaminated, spoiled, tainted, harmful, injurious, unfavorable, defective, inferior, imperfect, substandard, faulty, improper, inappropriate, unsuitable, disagreeable, unpleasant, cross, nasty, unfriendly, irascible, horrible, atrocious, outrageous, scandalous, infamous, wrong, noxious, sinister, putrid, snide, deplorable, dismal, gross, heinous, nefarious, base, obnoxious, detestable, despicable, contemptible, foul, rank, ghastly, execrable.

Beautiful — pretty, lovely, handsome, attractive, gorgeous, dazzling, splendid, magnificent, comely, fair, ravishing, graceful, elegant, fine, exquisite, aesthetic, pleasing, shapely, delicate, stunning, glorious, heavenly, resplendent, radiant, glowing, blooming, sparkling.

Begin — start, open, launch, initiate, commence, inaugurate, originate.

Big — enormous, huge, immense, gigantic, vast, colossal, gargantuan, large, sizable, grand, great, tall, substantial, mammoth, astronomical, ample, broad, expansive, spacious, stout, tremendous, titanic, mountainous.

Brave — courageous, fearless, dauntless, intrepid, plucky, daring, heroic, valorous, audacious, bold, gallant, valiant, doughty, mettlesome.

Break — fracture, rupture, shatter, smash, wreck, crash, demolish, atomize.

Bright — shining, shiny, gleaming, brilliant, sparkling, shimmering, radiant, vivid, colorful, lustrous, luminous, incandescent, intelligent, knowing, quick-witted, smart, intellectual.

Calm — quiet, peaceful, still, tranquil, mild, serene, smooth, composed, collected, unruffled, level-headed, unexcited, detached, aloof.

Come — approach, advance, near, arrive, reach.

Cool — chilly, cold, frosty, wintry, icy, frigid.

Crooked — bent, twisted, curved, hooked, zigzag.

Cry — shout, yell, yowl, scream, roar, bellow, weep, wail, sob, bawl

Cut — gash, slash, prick, nick, sever, slice, carve, cleave, slit, chop, crop, lop, reduce.

Dangerous — perilous, hazardous, risky, uncertain, unsafe.

Dark — shadowy, unlit, murky, gloomy, dim, dusky, shaded, sunless, black, dismal, sad.

Decide — determine, settle, choose, resolve.

Definite — certain, sure, positive, determined, clear, distinct, obvious.

Delicious — savory, delectable, appetizing, luscious, scrumptious, palatable, delightful, enjoyable, toothsome, exquisite.

Describe — portray, characterize, picture, narrate, relate, recount, represent, report, record.

Destroy — ruin, demolish, raze, waste, kill, slay, end, extinguish.

Difference — disagreement, inequity, contrast, dissimilarity, incompatibility.

Do — execute, enact, carry out, finish, conclude, effect, accomplish, achieve, attain.

Dull — boring, tiring, tiresome, uninteresting, slow, dumb, stupid, unimaginative, lifeless, dead, insensible, tedious, wearisome, listless, expressionless, plain, monotonous, humdrum, dreary.

Eager — keen, fervent, enthusiastic, involved, interested, alive to.

End — stop, finish, terminate, conclude, close, halt, cessation, discontinuance.

Enjoy — appreciate, delight in, be pleased, indulge in, luxuriate in, bask in, relish, devour, savor, like.

Explain — elaborate, clarify, define, interpret, justify, account for.

Fair — just, impartial, unbiased, objective, unprejudiced, honest.

Fall — drop, descend, plunge, topple, tumble.

False — fake, fraudulent, counterfeit, spurious, untrue, unfounded, erroneous, deceptive, groundless, fallacious.

Famous — well-known, renowned, celebrated, famed, eminent, illustrious, distinguished, noted, notorious.

Fast — quick, rapid, speedy, fleet, hasty, snappy, mercurial, swiftly, rapidly, quickly, snappily, speedily, lickety-split, posthaste, hastily, expeditiously, like a flash.

Fat — stout, corpulent, fleshy, beefy, paunchy, plump, full, rotund, tubby, pudgy, chubby, chunky, burly, bulky, elephantine.

Fear — fright, dread, terror, alarm, dismay, anxiety, scare, awe, horror, panic, apprehension.

Fly — soar, hover, flit, wing, flee, waft, glide, coast, skim, sail, cruise.

Funny — humorous, amusing, droll, comic, comical, laughable, silly.

Get — acquire, obtain, secure, procure, gain, fetch, find, score, accumulate, win, earn, rep, catch, net, bag, derive, collect, gather, glean, pick up, accept, come by, regain, salvage.

Go — recede, depart, fade, disappear, move, travel, proceed.

Good — excellent, fine, superior, wonderful, marvelous, qualified, suited, suitable, apt, proper, capable, generous, kindly, friendly, gracious, obliging, pleasant, agreeable, pleasurable, satisfactory, well-behaved, obedient, honorable, reliable, trustworthy, safe, favorable, profitable, advantageous, righteous, expedient, helpful, valid, genuine, ample, salubrious, estimable, beneficial, splendid, great, noble, worthy, first-rate, top-notch, grand, sterling, superb, respectable, edifying.

Great — noteworthy, worthy, distinguished, remarkable, grand, considerable, powerful, much, mighty.

Gross — improper, rude, coarse, indecent, crude, vulgar, outrageous, extreme, grievous, shameful, uncouth, obscene, low.

Happy — pleased, contented, satisfied, delighted, elated, joyful, cheerful, ecstatic, jubilant, gay, tickled, gratified, glad, blissful, overjoyed.

Hate — despise, loathe, detest, abhor, disfavor, dislike, disapprove, abominate.

Have — hold, possess, own, contain, acquire, gain, maintain, believe, bear, beget, occupy, absorb, fill, enjoy.

Help — aid, assist, support, encourage, back, wait on, attend, serve, relieve, succor, benefit, befriend, abet.

Hide — conceal, cover, mask, cloak, camouflage, screen, shroud, veil.

Hurry — rush, run, speed, race, hasten, urge, accelerate, bustle.

Hurt — damage, harm, injure, wound, distress, afflict, pain.

Idea — thought, concept, conception, notion, understanding, opinion, plan, view, belief.

Important — necessary, vital, critical, indispensable, valuable, essential, significant, primary, principal, considerable, famous, distinguished, notable, well-known.

Interesting — fascinating, engaging, sharp, keen, bright, intelligent, animated, spirited, attractive, inviting, intriguing, provocative, though-provoking, challenging, inspiring, involving, moving, titillating, tantalizing, exciting, entertaining, piquant, lively, racy, spicy, engrossing, absorbing, consuming, gripping, arresting, enthralling, spellbinding, curious, captivating, enchanting, bewitching, appealing.

Keep — hold, retain, withhold, preserve, maintain, sustain, support.

Kill — slay, execute, assassinate, murder, destroy, cancel, abolish.

Lazy — indolent, slothful, idle, inactive, sluggish.

Little — tiny, small, diminutive, shrimp, runt, miniature, puny, exiguous, dinky, cramped, limited, itsy-bitsy, microscopic, slight, petite, minute.

Look — gaze, see, glance, watch, survey, study, seek, search for, peek, peep, glimpse, stare, contemplate, examine, gape, ogle, scrutinize, inspect, leer, behold, observe, view, witness, perceive, spy, sight, discover, notice, recognize, peer, eye, gawk, peruse, explore.

Love — like, admire, esteem, fancy, care for, cherish, adore, treasure, worship, appreciate, savor.

Make — create, originate, invent, beget, form, construct, design, fabricate, manufacture, produce, build, develop, do, effect, execute, compose, perform, accomplish, earn, gain, obtain, acquire, get.

Mark — label, tag, price, ticket, impress, effect, trace, imprint, stamp, brand, sign, note, heed, notice, designate.

Mischievous — prankish, playful, naughty, roguish, waggish, impish, sportive.

Move — plod, go, creep, crawl, inch, poke, drag, toddle, shuffle, trot, dawdle, walk, traipse, mosey, jog, plug, trudge, slump, lumber, trail, lag, run, sprint, trip, bound, hotfoot, high-tail, streak, stride, tear, breeze, whisk, rush, dash, dart, bolt, fling, scamper, scurry, skedaddle, scoot, scuttle, scramble, race, chase, hasten, hurry, hump, gallop, lope, accelerate, stir, budge, travel, wander, roam, journey, trek, ride, spin, slip, glide, slide, slither, coast, flow, sail, saunter, hobble, amble, stagger, paddle, slouch, prance, straggle, meander, perambulate, waddle, wobble, pace, swagger, promenade, lunge.

Moody — temperamental, changeable, short-tempered, glum, morose, sullen, mopish, irritable, testy, peevish, fretful, spiteful, sulky, touchy.

Neat — clean, orderly, tidy, trim, dapper, natty, smart, elegant, well-organized, super, desirable, spruce, shipshape, well-kept, shapely.

New — fresh, unique, original, unusual, novel, modern, current, recent.

Old — feeble, frail, ancient, weak, aged, used, worn, dilapidated, ragged, faded, broken-down, former, old-fashioned, outmoded, passé, veteran, mature, venerable, primitive, traditional, archaic, conventional, customary, stale, musty, obsolete, extinct.

Part — portion, share, piece, allotment, section, fraction, fragment.

Place — space, area, spot, plot, region, location, situation, position, residence, dwelling, set, site, station, status, state.

Plan — plot, scheme, design, draw, map, diagram, procedure, arrangement, intention, device, contrivance, method, way, blueprint.

Popular — well-liked, approved, accepted, favorite, celebrated, common, current.

Predicament — quandary, dilemma, pickle, problem, plight, spot, scrape, jam.

Put — place, set, attach, establish, assign, keep, save, set aside, effect, achieve, do, build.

Quiet — silent, still, soundless, mute, tranquil, peaceful, calm, restful.

Right — correct, accurate, factual, true, good, just, honest, upright, lawful, moral, proper, suitable, apt, legal, fair.

Run — race, speed, hurry, hasten, sprint, dash, rush, escape, elope, flee.

Say/Tell — inform, notify, advise, relate, recount, narrate, explain, reveal, disclose, divulge, declare, command, order, bid, enlighten, instruct, insist, teach, train, direct, issue, remark, converse, speak, affirm, suppose, utter, negate, express, verbalize, voice, articulate, pronounce, deliver, convey, impart, assert, state, allege, mutter, mumble, whisper, sigh, exclaim, yell, sing, yelp, snarl, hiss, grunt, snort, roar, bellow, thunder, boom, scream, shriek, screech, squawk, whine, philosophize, stammer, stutter, lisp, drawl, jabber, protest, announce, swear, vow, content, assure, deny, dispute.

Scared — afraid, frightened, alarmed, terrified, panicked, fearful, unnerved, insecure, timid, shy, skittish, jumpy, disquieted, worried, vexed, troubled, disturbed, horrified, terrorized, shocked, petrified, haunted, timorous, shrinking, tremulous, stupefied, paralyzed, stunned, apprehensive.

Show — display, exhibit, present, note, point to, indicate, explain, reveal, prove, demonstrate, expose.

Slow — unhurried, gradual, leisurely, late, behind, tedious, slack.

Stop — cease, halt, stay, pause, discontinue, conclude, end, finish, quit.

Story — tale, myth, legend, fable, yarn, account, narrative, chronicle, epic, sage, anecdote, record, memoir.

Strange — odd, peculiar, unusual, unfamiliar, uncommon, queer, weird, outlandish, curious, unique, exclusive, irregular.

Take — hold, catch, seize, grasp, win, capture, acquire, pick, choose, select, prefer, remove, steal, lift, rob, engage, bewitch, purchase, buy, retract, recall, assume, occupy, consume.

Tell — disclose, reveal, show, expose, uncover, relate, narrate, inform, advise, explain, divulge, declare, command, order, bid, recount, repeat.

Think — judge, deem, assume, believe, consider, contemplate, reflect, mediate.

Trouble — distress, anguish, anxiety, worry, wretchedness, pain, danger, peril, disaster, grief, misfortune, difficulty, concern, pains, inconvenience, exertion, effort.

True — accurate, right, proper, precise, exact, valid, genuine, real, actual, trusty, steady, loyal, dependable, sincere, staunch.

Ugly — hideous, frightful, frightening, shocking, horrible, unpleasant, monstrous, terrifying, gross, grisly, ghastly, horrid, unsightly, plain, homely, evil, repulsive, repugnant, gruesome.

Unhappy — miserable, uncomfortable, wretched, heart-broken, unfortunate, poor, downhearted, sorrowful, depressed, dejected, melancholy, glum, gloomy, dismal, discouraged, sad.

Use — employ, utilize, exhaust, spend, expend, consume, exercise.

Wrong — incorrect, inaccurate, mistaken, erroneous, improper, unsuitable.

Words don't come easy

When we speak, we convey our emotions with more than just words. Body language is one way we do this. Another is through a character's voice. For example, a woman speaking in a smoky-sounding voice will come across as sexy and alluring. Here is a selection from **writinghelpers** (http://writinghelpers.tumblr.com):

- **Breathy**: a breathy voice may signify excitement or desire.
- **Brittle**: a brittle voice signifies a character who is about to cry.
- **Booming**: very loud and attention-getting.
- **Croaky**: if someone's voice sounds croaky, they speak in a low, rough voice that sounds as if they have a sore throat.
- **Flat**: spoken in a voice that does not go up and down.
- **Grating**: a grating voice, laugh, or sound is unpleasant and annoying.
- **Gravelly**: a gravelly voice sounds low and rough.
- **Gruff**: this voice has a rough, low sound.
- **Guttural**: a guttural sound is deep and made at the back of your throat.
- **High-pitched**: true to its name, a high-pitched voice or sound is very high.
- **Hoarse**: someone who is hoarse, or has a hoarse voice, speaks in a low, rough voice, usually because their throat is sore.
- **Honeyed**: honeyed words or a honeyed voice sound very nice, but you cannot trust the person who is speaking.

- **Husky**: a husky voice is deep and sounds hoarse (as if you have a sore throat), often in an attractive way.
- **Low**: a low voice is quiet and difficult to hear; also used for describing a deep voice that has a long wavelength.
- **Matter-of-fact**: usually used if the person speaking knows what they are talking about (or absolutely think they know what they are talking about).
- **Monotonous**: this kind of voice is boring and unpleasant due to the fact that it does not change in loudness or become higher/lower.
- **Nasal**: someone with a nasal voice sounds as if they are speaking through their nose.
- **Penetrating**: a penetrating voice is so high or loud that it makes you slightly uncomfortable.
- **Raucous**: a raucous voice or noise is loud and sounds rough.
- **Ringing**: a ringing voice is very loud and clear.
- **Rough**: a rough voice is not soft and is unpleasant to listen to.
- **Shrill**: a shrill voice is very loud, high, and unpleasant.
- **Silvery**: this voice is clear, light, and pleasant.
- **Singsong**: if you speak in a singsong voice, your voice rises and falls in a musical way.
- **Smoky**: a smoky voice is sexually attractive in a slightly mysterious way.
- **Soft**: someone who is soft-spoken has a quiet, gentle voice.
- **Stentorian**: a stentorian voice sounds very loud and severe.
- **Strangled**: a strangled sound is one that someone stops before they finish making it.
- **Taut**: used about something such as a voice that shows someone is nervous or angry.

- **Thick**: your voice is thick with an emotion.
- **Throaty**: a throaty sound is low and seems to come from deep in your throat.
- **Tight**: shows that you are nervous or annoyed.
- **Tremulous**: if your voice is tremulous, it is not steady; for example, because you are afraid or excited.
- **In an undertone**: using a quiet voice so that someone cannot hear you.
- **Wheezy**: a wheezy noise sounds as if it is made by someone who has difficulty breathing.
- **Whispery**: using a quiet voice so that someone cannot hear you.
- **Wobbly**: if your voice is wobbly, it goes up and down, usually because you are frightened, not confident, or about to cry.
- **Quavering**: if your voice quavers, it is not steady because you are feeling nervous or afraid.

Sensory Words

Author **Sue Coletta** has shared the following list of sensory verbs, compiled by **Cristina Malinn**. These verbs are a great way of bringing immediacy to your descriptions.

Hearing

Loud	Soft	Speech
Crash	Whisper	Stammer
Thunder	Sigh	Giggle
Yell	Murmur	Guffaw
Blare	Snap	Laugh
Thud	Patter	Sing
Boom	Swish	Scream
Bang	Giggle	Screech
Smash	Sing	Snort
Explode	Snort	Bellow
Roar	Chatter	Growl
Scream	Drawl	Chatter
Screech	Whisper	Murmur
Shout	Whir	Whisper
Whistle	Rustle	Whimper
Whine	Twitter	Talk
Squawk	Patter	Speak
Bark	Hum	Drawl

Bawl	Mutter	
Bray	Snap	
Rage	Hiss	
Grate	Crackle	
Slam	Bleat	
Clap	Peep	
Stomp	Buzz	
Stamp	Zing	
Jangle	Gurgle	
Clash	Rush	
Deafening	Chime	
Pierce	Tinkle	
	Clink	
	Hush	

Other Senses

Touch	Taste	Smell	Sight
Cool	Oily	Sweet	Dark
Cold	Buttery	Scented	Dismal
Icy	Salty	Fragrant	Rotted
Lukewarm	Bitter	Aromatic	Old
Tepid	Bittersweet	Perfumed	Used
Warm	Sweet	Heady	Worn
Hot	Hearty	Fresh	Untidy
Steamy	Mellow	Balmy	Shabby
Sticky	Sugary	Earthy	Messy
Damp	Crisp	Piney	Cheap
Wet	Ripe	Odorous	Ugly

Slippery	Bland	Pungent	Ramshackle
Spongy	Tasteless	Tempting	Tired
Mushy	Sour	Spicy	Exhausted
Oily	Vinegary	Savory	Arid
Waxy	Fruity	Sharp	Awkward
Fleshy	Tangy	Gamy	Crooked
Rubbery	Unripe	Fishy	Loose
Tough	Raw	Briny	Curved
Crisp	Alkaline	Acidy	Straight
Elastic	Medicinal	Acrid	Orderly
Leathery	Fishy	Burnt	Formal
Silky	Spicy	Gaseous	Crisp
Satiny	Peppery	Reeking	Pretty
Velvety	Gingery	Putrid	Heavy
Smooth	Hot	Rotten	Flat
Soft	Burnt	Spoiled	Stout
Woolly	Overripe	Sour	Wide
Furry	Spoiled	Rancid	Rigid
Feathery	Rotten	Sickly	Narrow
Fuzzy		Stagnant	Overloaded
Hairy		Moldy	Congested
Prickly		Musty	Cluttered
Gritty		Mildewed	Crowded
Sandy		Damp	Jammed
Rough		Dank	Packed
Sharp		Stench	Bruised
Thick			Tied
Pulpy			Stretched
Dry			Tall

Dull			Erect
Thin			Lean
Fragile			Slender
Tender			Supple

Movement

Fast	Slow
Hurry	Creep
Run	Crawl
Scamper	Plod
Skip	Slouch
Scramble	Lumber
Dart	Tiptoe
Spring	Bend
Spin	Amble
Stride	Saunter
Streak	Loiter
Propel	Stray
Trot	Slink
Gallop	Stalk
Drive	Edge
Dash	Sneak
Bolt	Stagger
Careen	Lope
Rush	Canter
Race	Waddle
Zoom	Drag

Zip	Sway
Ram	Soar
Speed	Lift
Chase	Drift
Hurl	Droop
Swat	Heave
Flick	
Whisk	
Rip	
Shove	
Swerve	
Smash	
Drop	
Plummet	
Bounce	
Dive	
Swoop	
Plunge	
Swing	
Fly	
Sail	

Other sensory words

Lithe	Wild	Showy
Lively	Bold	Decorative
Muscular	Dramatic	Dazzling
Sturdy	Tantalizing	Opulent
Robust	Irresistible	Jeweled
Hardy	Energetic	Lavish
Strong	Animated	Exotic
Healthy	Perky	Radiant
Frail	Arrogant	Fiery
Fragile	Imposing	Blazing
Pale	Regal	Fresh
Sickly	Stately	Clean
Small	Elegant	Scrubbed
Tiny	Large	Tidy
Miniature	Huge	Handsome
Timid	Immense	Pleasant
Shy	Massive	Calm
Nervous	Gigantic	Serene
Frightened		

Using Smell

Author **Rayne Hall** has the following suggestions when it comes to smell:

- The place reeked/stank of AAA and BBB.
- The odours of AAA and BBB mingled with the smells of CCC and DDD.
- Her nostrils detected a whiff of AAA beneath the smells of BBB and CCC.
- The smell of AAA warred with the stronger odour of BBB.
- The air was rich with the scents of AAA and BBB.
- The smell of AAA failed to mask the stench of BBB.
- The stench of AAA hit him first, followed by the odour of BBB.
- Beneath the scent of AAA lay the more ominous odours of BBB and CCC.
- The scents of AAA and BBB greeted her.
- The smells of AAA and BBB made his mouth water.
- He braced himself against the stink of AAA and BBB.
- The sweet sting of gas knifed into his nose.
- His nostrils flared.
- (Smell) attacked his nostrils.

Examples by Christine Plouvier

The examples below are taken from Christine Plouvier's novel, *The Irish Firebrands.*

- On the hearth, there burnt a small fire that smelt of apple wood.

- He ground out words as stale as the indoor air.

- The very smell of his unfinished pint was so bitter it made him faint with nausea before he could put it to his lips.

- He lost himself in the scent of her hair, the warmth of her body, the sound of her breathing.

- Her crockery bowls warmed on the iron cooker, filled with steamy, creamy potatoes flecked with bright green onions and surrounding deep golden wells of melted butter.

- She brought an aura of fresh cigarette smoke into the room. The glances exchanged by the other students indicated they noticed it, too.

- She caught a whiff of smoke. It rapidly grew stronger and had an almost incense-like quality.

- She recoiled from alleyways that reeked of urine and echoed with retching.

- The aroma of frying bacon lured her to the archway.

- She had expected the farmyard to be muddy and malodorous, but the earth turned out to be hard-packed, pebbly clay, and the odor of ordure was muted.

- She was enveloped in an aura of pipe tobacco that clung to a thin, soft shirt veiling warm, hard muscles—and for one mad moment, it was the fragrance of heaven.

- The shop exuded a musty, dusty smell.
- The cloudburst swept down the street and the scent of rain wafted in, freshening the ancient atmosphere that seeped from the building.
- He cried himself to sleep on her scented satin bosom.
- He was so close, she caught a whiff of his shaving soap and thought of his old-fashioned mug and brush on his bathroom shelf.
- By the time that task had been completed, the air had filled with the autumnal aroma of stewing apples.
- The air was redolent with the aroma of food and resonant with the chatter of women who were arranging platters and bowls upon the worktops.
- He inhaled deeply above the first spoonful. "It smells like Mom's pies!"
- He awoke to the scent of fresh-baked cinnamon-sultana scones.
- She snuggled into the blankets with a fragrantly steaming mug close at hand.
- The spicy scent was so strong, that the pie couldn't have been very long out of the oven—indeed, warmth still radiated from it.
- She locked herself into the flat, and then leaned against the door with her eyes shut, savoring the faint, familiar scent that would always mean – *Him!*
- Picking up a pillow from the tumbled bed, he held it to his cheek. The cool linen still held the fragrance that to him would always mean – *Her!*

- She grasped a woolly fold and held it to her cheek. Its warm, soft prickliness evoked a fantasy of snuggling against his strong chest but the aura she sought was too faint.

- His scent on the pillow seduced her into staying the night in his flat.

- An egg of unknown vintage but that still smelled fresh, and milk from an unfinished liter that had passed its pull date, went into making buttered pancakes for her supper.

- She had fantasies of lingering lovemaking upon scented sheets bathed in magic moonlight.

- He was aware of her warm body in his arms, her soft, scented cheek against his own and her husky laughter in his ear.

- Thick tobacco smoke had sullied the air by the time she re-entered the house.

- The reek of urine and rotting rubbish on a damp December night surrounded her.

- To protect his eyes, he pressed his face against her soft flesh, where he breathed deeply of the scent of her skin – and for one mad moment, it was the fragrance of heaven.

- That first intimate moment was intoxicating: the clean, wet smell of his skin, the softness of his damp chest hair against her cheek, the feeling of him in her arms, his living, breathing, heart pounding under her lips—and she could no longer fight her desire for him.

- The air was filled with the scents and sounds of the early spring night: damp earth, frogs' peeping serenade, a tinkling bell in some faraway sheepfold, the whiff of peat smoke; all so achingly beautiful.

- His last day there was gusty, good for drying bedclothes, and his final task was to remake the four-poster bed with wind-freshened sheets and duvet cover.
- A filthy calf had once stepped inside, and the everlasting stench of manure now gave her a migraine.

More Professional Examples

The following examples show how some other authors have used this technique in their fiction.

- The room smelled like stale smoke and Italian salad dressing. (Michael Connelly: The Poet)
- I took a couple of deep breaths, smelled rain, diesel and the pungent dead-fish-and-salt stench off the river. (Devon Monk: Magic to the Bone)
- The place smelt of damp and decay. (Jonathan Stroud: The Amulet of Samarkand)
- A rare south wind had brought the smell of Tyre to last night's landfall: cinnamon and pepper in the cedar-laced pine smoke, sharp young wine and close-packed sweating humanity, smouldering hemp and horse piss. (Mathew Woodring Stover: Iron Dawn)
- The smell hit her first: rotting flesh, ancient blood. (Kristine Kathryn Rusch: Sins of the Blood)
- The air reeked of hot metal, overheated electronic components, scorched insulation – and gasoline. (D. Koontz: The Bad Place)
- The air held the warm odours of honey and earth, of pine resin and goat sweat, mingled with the scents of frying oil and spice. (Rayne Hall: Storm Dancer)
- As the off cuts fell into the dust below they released the smell of new timber that was like spring (Philippa Rees: Blerie Fockin)

- I pulled in a breath, savored that heavy tang of ancient earth mingled with long-standing water (Beem Weeks: Jazz Baby)

Ways to Describe Crying

Blooming Azaleas of **QuoteTV** has compiled the following list of ways to describe crying, and the differences between them:

- **Bawling:** Noisy crying, usually with whining and/or heavy breathing.
- **Blubbering:** Unattractive, loud crying. Characterized by mutters, truncated, erratic breathing, clinched facial expressions and hunched posture.
- **Crying:** The act of distress when tears (usually) appear.
- **Hyperventilate-Crying:** Forceful crying causing heavy breathing, resulting in the inability to speak or produce sounds even resembling words.
- **Scream-Crying:** Violent crying accompanied with bouts of yelling or sometimes shrieking. May also include slapping, punching or other physical expressions of distress.
- **Silent Tears:** Soft, inaudible crying that does not draw attention. May manifest only in a single tear rolling down one's cheek (a beat, however, that is considered overdone in literature).
- **Sniffling:** The act of sniffling repeatedly when crying, usually after a big crying fit.
- **Sniveling:** Audible, but soft crying, also prone to muttering and erratic breathing; May also show signs of drool or mucus.

- **Sobbing**: Heavy crying with a large volume tears flowing steadily. Generally audible but not inappropriately loud.
- **Weeping:** A gentler version of sobbing; Involves soft, steady stream of tears with some times lightly audible signs of distress.
- **Whimpering:** Soft crying usually including few or no tears at all. It often incorporates muttering and/or high-pitched sighs.

Types of Crying

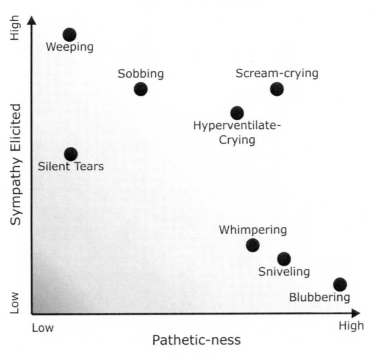

Ways to Describe Snoring

Author **Charles E. Yallowitz** has come up with these nice similes that cover snoring.

He snores like…

- a goose getting strangled underwater.
- running chainsaw put through a woodchipper.
- gargling mouthwash.
- standard sawing of log.
- a choking thing that makes me think she's in trouble.
- the gasp from a dramatic movie that requires you put your hand to your chest.
- a baby elephant blowing bubbles in chocolate milk.
- a tweety bird.

Ways to Describe Writing

Author **Lucy Mitchell (aka Blondewritemore)** has come up with these exciting ways of describing her writing progress:

- "Tonight I wrote 456 words!"
- "Today I nailed 1,290 words!"
- "This afternoon I banged out 1,456 words!"
- "I only managed to cobble together 45 words today"
- "I scraped together 100 words this afternoon"
- "Today I conjured up 2,500 words!"
- "Tonight I rattled off 567 words!"
- "This morning I whipped up 800 words!"
- "Today I pumped out 765 words!"
- "Tonight I hammered home 987 words!"
- "I churned out 309 words!"
- "Today I could only squeeze out 154 words"
- "This afternoon 1,300 words gushed out of me!"
- "Today I belted out 1,899 words!"
- "Today I pounded out 1,900 words"
- "This afternoon I blew past my goal with 1,300 words"
- "This morning I coughed up 456 words"
- "Today 2,300 words shot out of me"
- "Boom!" (exploding fist hand action) "2,090 words!"

Acknowledgments

Among many others, this book contains beats by:

- Alicia Dean
- Angela Ackerman
- Beem Weeks
- Blondewritemore
- Charles E. Yallowitz
- Cristina Mallin
- Christine Plouvier
- C.S. Lakin
- D. Wallace Peach
- David Wind
- Don Massenzio
- Eamon Gosney
- Elizabeth George
- Elle Boca
- Jennifer Owenby
- Lara Eakins
- MacMillan Dictionary (visit for more ways to describe looks)
- Mark Nichol
- MMJaye
- Paula Cappa
- QuoteTV

- <u>Rayne Hall</u>
- <u>Sue Coletta</u>
- <u>WriteWorld</u> (click for more alternatives to "walking")
- <u>Writing Helpers</u> (click for more ways to describe voices)

The definition of Emotional Beats comes from the Writer's Digest article, <u>How to Amp up Dialogue with Emotional Beats</u> by Todd A. Stone.

Thank you for sharing your beautiful words with us.

I am also grateful to <u>Elle Boca</u>, <u>D.G. Kaye</u>, <u>Maria Messini</u>, <u>Rachael Ritchey</u>, and Gabriele for pointing out the mistakes in the original manuscript.

Once again, I have <u>Alex Saskalidis</u> and <u>Dimitris Fousekis</u> to thank for their beautiful art. I should also mention all fellow Indie authors—I know how hard it is what you do—and my wonderful social media followers.

To them, to my wife, my parents, and to the many teachers who have taught me so much in this life, as well as to my readers, without whose support this endeavor would matter but little, I offer my deep gratitude.

About the author

Nicholas Rossis lives to write and does so from his cottage on the edge of a magical forest in Athens, Greece. When not composing epic fantasies or short sci-fi stories, he chats with fans and colleagues, writes blog posts, walks his dog, and enjoys the antics of two silly cats and his daughter, all of whom claim his lap as home.

Nicholas is all around the Internet, but the best place to connect with him would be on his blog, http://nicholasrossis.me/

You can check out his books on Amazon: http://author.to/rossis

Notes from the author

Also available from Nicholas C. Rossis:

- **Pearseus**
  Could You Save The Woman Who Killed Your Son? Described as "Ancient Greece—in space," this best-selling science fiction/fantasy that was picked as one of the *100 Indie books you must read before you die* is available on Amazon: http://mybook.to/Pearseus

- **Award-winning short Science Fiction / Speculative Fiction stories**
  Now available on Amazon: http://myBook.to/ssf

- **Award-winning children's books:** Check them out for free on http://nicholasrossis.me/childrens-books
  - **Runaway Smile: an unshared smile is a wasted smile**. A little boy's smile runs away until it owner learns that an unshared smile is a wasted smile. *Runaway Smile* has won numerous awards. It is available on Amazon: http://myBook.to/smile.

  - **Musiville: let's face the music and... conduct**. An award-winning, music-filled children's book. Available on Amazon: http://myBook.to/musiville .

All books are free on Kindle Unlimited.

Want to contact me? Eager for updates? Want an e-book autograph? Please follow me on:

- http://nicholasrossis.me
- https://twitter.com/Nicholas_Rossis
- https://www.facebook.com/NicholasCRossis

If you wish to report a typo or have reviewed this book on Amazon please email info@nicholasrossis.com with the word "review" on the subject line, to receive a free 1680x1050 desktop background.

Other copyright:
1000 Verbs to Write was written by Alicia Dean
Describing Death was written by D. Wallace Peach
How Do I Look was compiled in part from a list found in MacMillan
Dictionary. © Macmillan Publishers Limited 2009–2016.
List of Common Synonyms was written by Lara Eakins
Sensory Words were compiled by Cristina Malinn and shared by Sue
Coletta
Using smell was written by Rayne Hall
Using smell examples by Christine Plouvier were taken from Christine
Plouvier's novel, *The Irish Firebrands*
Walking and Moving (II) was compiled in part from a list found on
WriteWorld
Ways to Describe Crying was compiled in part from a list by Blooming
Azaleas of QuoteTV
Ways to Describe Snoring was written by Charles E. Yallowitz
Ways to Describe Writing was written by Lucy Mitchell (aka
Blondewritemore)
Words don't come easy was compiled in part from a list found on
writinghelpers

Thank you for taking the time to read *Emotional Beats*! If you enjoyed it, please tell your friends or post a short review. Word of mouth is an author's best friend and much appreciated!

Made in United States
North Haven, CT
01 March 2024

49407270R10119